The Intended Christian Life

Living a Life of Purpose, Power, Authority, and Righteousness

D1563239

Steve Dominguez

ISBN: 1499541678
ISBN 13: 9781499541670

Dedication

I dedicate this book first and foremost to my Lord Jesus Christ. I love you, and I thank you for how you have sought me out and have drawn me into a deeper understanding of who you are.

In addition, I dedicate this book to my wife Risa who has been right along my side on this awesome journey. You have made the experience twice as fun.

Lastly, I dedicate this book to my wonderful children, Daniel, Amy, and Stephen. I'm very blessed to be your father. It's amazing to me how real your faith is to you all and how faithful you all are in using the gifts God has blessed you with. Thank you for passing the torch to the next generation to come.

I also want to give a special thanks to my parents for raising me in a Christian home and starting our family on the right track.

Endorsements

"Steve Dominguez' new book, **The Intended Christian Life**, is filled with excellent insights and teachings that obviously flow out from the heart and mind of someone thoroughly grounded in Scripture and who walks in the experiences that he writes about. I really appreciate his focus on the goodness and compassion of God, the authority of the believer, the release of God's presence and power through worship, the personhood of the Holy Spirit, and much, much more. I highly recommend this book!"

Dr. Clayton Ford
National Chair of Holy Spirit Renewal Ministries

"I am so encouraged after reading this book! Steve and Risa are true purebreds for the Kingdom of God. I know you will also be moved and blessed."

Angela T. Greenig
Founder of Angela Greenig Ministries
Author, *Armed and Dangerous*

"It is a huge honor to endorse Steve Dominguez and his work, **The Intended Christian Life**. I have known Steve and his wife Risa for a few years now. Something that really impresses me about these two is that they not only have a wonderful message that they speak verbally, but they live a life saturated with miracles, love, and power. I have seen Steve personally pursue a Jesus-fashioned lifestyle to see the kingdom of God come through his life to touch others.

I am excited about this fresh work of Steve's heart. This book is small, but power packed. It hits many powerful truths about living a power-filled Christian life with such clarity. He also attacks many commonly believed lies that would try to keep us from living in our proper identity in Christ.

I love how simple, yet profound, this book is. You will surely be challenged, encouraged, inspired, and more activated to live THE INTENDED CHRISTIAN LIFE."

Jason Chin
Author, *LOVESAYSGO*

Table of Contents

Introduction

The reason I chose the title <u>The Intended Christian Life</u> is because most of us are not living the life Christ intended. In fact, we even have lost sight and understanding of the life God intended. I thought I was living the intended Christian life, but I was missing one significant ingredient: power. Now to be honest, I moved in little, itsy bitsy sized power. However, when I read the book of Acts, I see my power is insignificant when compared to that of the early church leaders.

I also was not following the intent of the great commission. When people think of the great commission, they typically think of two things: preach the gospel/evangelize, make disciples. I was doing these two things to some extent, but there is more to the great commission than that.

First off, we know teaching is a part of discipleship and is explicitly stated in the great commission. So, what are we to teach? Does it say, "teaching to observe all things that I taught you?" No, it says, "teaching to observe all things that I *commanded* you." What's the difference? A commandment, verses a teaching, implies action. We do way too much teaching that is all about facts, but lacks any action. This, in turn, creates a culture of discipleship which is just teaching each other facts and concepts, but lacks role modeling this in everyday life.

What did Jesus tell His disciples to do? He sent them to preach the kingdom of God, heal the sick, raise the dead, and cast out demons.

> Luke 9:2
> He sent them to preach the kingdom of God and to heal the sick.

> Matthew 10:7-8
> And as you go, preach, saying, 'The kingdom of heaven is at hand.' Heal the sick, cleanse the lepers, raise the dead, cast out demons. Freely you have received, freely give.

That being said, let me rephrase what the great commission is at its core. It is to teach people to heal the sick, raise the dead, cast out demons, and preach the kingdom of God. So, as we look at this, we need to honestly ask ourselves if we are fulfilling the great commission and living the intended Christian life.

What Does it Mean to be an Ambassador for Christy?

The great commission is our responsibility, and an ambassador for Christ is our position. We are Christians, Christ followers, little representatives of Christ. As Paul says in 2 Corinthians 5:20, we are to be ambassadors for Christ. So, what is an ambassador? The Webster Dictionary definition is "An authorized representative or messenger."

There are three key parts to the definition. We are authorized, we are representatives, and we are messengers. The ambassador represents and carries a message (and both are with the authority of who they represent). This is why for Christians, Jesus said in John 20:23, "If you forgive the sins of any, they are forgiven them; if you retain the sins of any, they are retained." We, of course, don't have the ability to forgive the penalty of sin. After all, their trespasses are against God. Only God can forgive sins. However, it shows the weight of the message we are commissioned to carry. This commission is once again highlighted in the previous two verses.

John 20:21-22
So Jesus said to them again, "Peace to you! As the Father has sent Me, I also send you." And when He had said this,

He breathed on them, and said to them, "Receive the Holy Spirit."

As can be seen, the context of that verse is in the disciple's commission. As His ambassadors, we carry the message of the gospel. It's a message we carry with authority and power. The power comes from the Holy Spirit which Jesus released on them as He gave the commission.

The message of the gospel we are told to give is that of the Kingdom of God. Part of that is forgiveness of our sins and salvation, but that is not the complete gospel. That is only the gospel of salvation. No doubt, that is the most important part. However, the full gospel is that of God's kingdom. God's kingdom is where God rules.

> 1 Peter 2:11
> Beloved, I beg you **as sojourners and pilgrims**, abstain from fleshly lusts which war against the soul,

> Philippians 3:20
> For **our citizenship is in heaven**, from which we also eagerly wait for the Savior, the Lord Jesus Christ,

We are foreigners, and according to the apostle Paul we are citizens of another place (heaven). This seems rather abstract and impractical. However, when we look at it from an ambassador point of view, Christians represent God in a foreign land. This view becomes important when we try to live the intended Christian life.

As we pursue the life as a disciple of Christ, we can't help but talk about healing because we see it throughout the gospels. Healing was an integral part of Jesus' and the disciples' ministry. It's also the most common place to see the glory of God, and it opens doors to the full gospel. It also brings life back to (revives) our faith. I know a lot of teenagers that are getting a taste of this, where they experience the reality of their faith in a tangible and powerful way. As a result, it's brought a fire into their lives. In turn, they have taken their life for Christ much more seriously and have led friends and relatives to the Lord.

Healing is also part of the full gospel and the great commission. When people are healed, they get a taste of God's kingdom. Now, of course, God didn't promise we would always be healed in this world. After all, we are all terminal, and His kingdom is not fully realized until He returns. However, it should be known that provision for healing was made in the atonement. Don't take my word for it. Isaiah and Matthew say so.

> Isaiah 53:4-5 (NIV)
> Surely He took up our pain and bore our suffering, yet we considered Him punished by God, stricken by Him, and afflicted. But He was pierced for our transgressions, He was crushed for our iniquities; the punishment that brought us peace was on Him, and by His wounds we are healed.

As the verse says, by His wounds we are healed. I used to think this was in a spiritual sense only, but when I read where this passage is quoted in Matthew, the context is that of physical healing.

> Matthew 8:16, 17 (NIV)
> When evening came, many who were demon-possessed were brought to him, and he drove out the spirits with a word and healed all the sick. This was to fulfill what was spoken through the prophet Isaiah:
> "He took up our infirmities and bore our diseases."

I know this raises many questions. Such as, if we are healed by His stripes, then why do Christians die in sickness? I know my answer will sound like a cop out, but I believe it to be the case. That is, all

Christians will be completely healed and made new in all areas, physically, mentally, emotionally, and spiritually. It's just a matter of time. When we Christians are in heaven, we will all be completely healed. However, we get tastes of God's kingdom here on earth because the work on the cross enables it to be possible now, but it is not always manifested. As we can see, this world does not fully reflect God's will. This is why Jesus prayed, "Your will be done on earth as it is in heaven." We as ambassadors are to help represent and help present the kingdom to come, but it's not here yet.

God's Will in Sickness

If we are representatives of God, we need to know God's will. A proper understanding of this is especially important in the area of sickness and trials because it is there that many views of God have gotten distorted. Understanding God's will in these areas will help lay a solid foundation of God's love and compassion.

In Mathew, Jesus prays the famous prayer in which He says, "Your will be done on earth as it is in heaven." This implies that 1) earth is not reflective of God's will and that 2) heaven is reflective of God's will. In heaven we see no pain, no sickness, etc. That's also how earth was created to be before the fall of man. That's God's will.

> Luke 5:12-13 (NIV)
> While Jesus was in one of the towns, a man came along who was covered with leprosy. When he saw Jesus, he fell with his face to the ground and begged him, "Lord, if you are willing, you can make me clean." Jesus reached out his hand and touched the man. "**I am willing**," he said. "Be clean!" And immediately the leprosy left him.

Jesus was willing to heal the leper, and He touched the man (it was more than just a physical healing). He showed complete compassion. While healings manifest the glory of God, they also show His will and His heart. It's critical that we understand His heart if we are to represent Him well.

One time when traveling on business, there was a lady wearing an orange bracelet sitting next to me on the plane. I felt God say to ask her about the bracelet, but I just couldn't muster up the courage. Then suddenly the plane dropped, in a free fall manner, for probably just a second, but it felt like a long time to my stomach. The drop was large enough to get the attention of most people on the plane, and it was perhaps the key that got me into a conversation with this lady. As the conversation took different turns, it came out that her teenage daughter was brutally murdered. The orange bracelet had a website address of an organization she and her husband founded after that tragedy to help address situations like theirs. I told her I'd be praying for her, and I shared some thoughts with her that I felt would be comforting. She later sought me out at baggage claim to say good bye and said she really appreciated our talk. One doesn't always need to say much in situations like that, just the right things. Proverbs 25:11 says, "A word fitly spoken is like apples of gold in pictures of silver."

So, how does one respond to that? That God is sovereign and that must have been His plan for her daughter? Very sadly, that is how some Christians think. To that, the obvious argument would be that sin is never God's will. So, can we all agree that things happen that are not God's will? We hopefully know His general will, that none should perish as it says in 2 Peter 3:9. Yet, we know that many will perish.

As we can see, our world doesn't reflect God's character. God is sovereign, but that doesn't mean everything is controlled by Him. This is often the toughest thing for Christians to understand. But, if everything is acting in perfect accordance with His will, then there would be no purpose to praying. It would have been all pre-decided. If God is controlling both sides of the battle of good and evil, what's the point?

His sovereignty means He has complete authority. He can choose to execute that authority, but man has been given free will. There is an expression: "kingdom now, but not yet." We are currently in God's kingdom spiritually, but not physically. However, we, as His representatives, have the privilege to carry His authority. So, until Christ returns, we live in a world where kingdoms collide. And that clash of kingdoms is often manifested physically.

When my sister Mary first got inflammatory breast cancer, I and a few others laid hands on her and prayed. This type of cancer is actually visibly manifested on the skin. So, we could know if our prayers were being answered. Early on, when it first showed up, we prayed, and all visible sign of cancer went away. It confused the doctors. In fact, the surgeon didn't even want to do the biopsy because we prayed between the time her doctor saw her and the surgeon saw her. When she saw the surgeon, she looked fine. So, it confused the doctors. Then it confused us as well because the signs of the cancer came back a day or two later. We prayed again and all visible signs of cancer went away in a matter of minutes. Then it came back again a day or two later. This cancer doesn't do that. It doesn't show up and go away.

This had the doctors confused, and it had us confused and frustrated. Twice it did this. I contemplated this. If it was God's will for the cancer to go away, why did it come back? If it wasn't God's will for her to be healed, why did it go away at all? I found that these questions would get me nowhere. So, I've learned to look at things from a different way, and a much more appropriate way, to help make sense of it all. It's very simple. We are in a war.

The fact is the end of the war was decided at Calvary when Christ died and rose again. However, until His return there are many battles to be fought, and Jesus left us with responsibility to fight those battles. Our prayers do make a difference. We need to get that in our heads and in our hearts to be effective in ministry. Whether we pray or not makes a difference. As Paul states in 1Corintians 3:9, "…we are co-workers in God's service…". We have a part to play.

Often, the only factors that Christians see when one is sick are the sickness, the sick person, and God. This short list often leads to a way of thinking that ends up creating bad theology. For example, what happens when a person doesn't get healed? Their list is very short. So, they conclude that it must be one of the following: it's God's will, the person lacks faith, or the person must have sin in his life.

I'm not saying that faith and sin aren't sometimes factors, but there is way more going on than we often realize. For example, as Daniel was interceding for Israel, he needed to wait for 21 days for his prayers to get answered due to the resistance.

Daniel 10:13 (NIV)
But the prince of the Persian kingdom resisted me twenty-one days. Then Michael, one of the chief princes, came to help me, because I was detained there with the king of Persia.

Satan brings resistance. He has an agenda. What does Jesus say in John 10:10? The enemy, that is Satan, has come to kill, steal, and destroy. Whenever we see loss, death, and destruction, we know that this is from the enemy. And it says in 1 John 3:8 that Jesus came to destroy the works for the devil. Again John 10:10 says, "The thief comes only to steal and kill and destroy; I have come that they may have life, and have it to the full."

I don't have all the answers, but I've learned this: Don't let circumstances, trials, and unanswered questions override what we know to be true. Trials have a tendency to do that though.

In the midst of the cancer, one of the things I commonly prayed for with my sister Mary was joy and a peace that goes beyond understanding. That is, there are no reasons for the peace or that joy. That's what makes it supernatural. There's no logic to it. Yet, James says to consider it all joy when faced with various trials. Trials can help with spiritual growth and create opportunities to see God's glory. Trials are useless to those intending to just live the American dream and will not bring joy. They only pray for the trial to leave. However, those with a warfare mindset know that trials are a normal part of the Christian life, and they pray for wisdom as James instructs them so they maneuver within them.

James says to consider. When we consider, we need to use our minds. We are challenged to think differently. And when we think, we need to start with what we know without a doubt to be true. That truth starts with what is clear from the God's Word. Let's not base our truth on speculation or theory such as God must be teaching me a lesson or punishing me. If God is punishing you, He'll make it obvious. Otherwise, it would be like a parent disciplining their child without telling the child what they did to deserve it. That would be ridiculous. Why is it we immediately place the blame on God when bad things happen? God uses all things, including tragedy, for our good. But that doesn't mean He causes them.

When Jesus was baptized by John the Baptist, what happened? Some paint a cute picture of a dove landing on Jesus. That's not quite the correct picture according to Matthew's version which, in fact, was a much more brilliant experience. John saw the Holy Spirit descend on Jesus like a dove and lighting on Him (Matthew 3:16). That's something one would remember. Secondly, a voice from heaven says, "This is my Son, whom I love; with him I am well pleased."

There was a lot of direct revelation. Before it all, John the Baptist himself proclaimed Jesus to be the Lamb of God (John 1:29). So, John must have even had it revealed to him as to who Jesus is even before he baptized Him and the amazing visual and audible things happened. Yet, when John is thrown in prison and awaiting execution, he sends his disciples to ask Jesus if He is the Messiah because his circumstances made him question what he knew to be true. Trials will do that. James says in James 1:3 that trials will test our faith. It's not our character being tested; it's our faith. When we are in a trial, the circumstances we are in the midst of will bring a lot of questions to our minds, but it's then that we need to stand on solid ground and on truth. Again, we can't let our unanswered questions override what we know to be true.

What then should we know for absolute certain? Two things: 1) God is good, and 2) God loves us, regardless of what our circumstances may make us question. This is critical to get in our hearts to live the effective and intended Christian life. If Satan can get us to question whether God is good or whether God really loves us, he can render us ineffective for God.

When Jesus walked the earth, it was clear that God heals. Most Christians believe God still can, but it's not expected. Instead, we tend these days to attribute sickness to God more than healing. Like God is trying to spiritually grow the sick people through the experience. While that may happen, God doesn't cause us to be sick to teach lessons or grow faith. As soon as a person starts to think that way, he will have a tainted view, no matter how hard he tries not to, of God and His love. We need to know that sickness is not God's will. We need to get back to the fact that, just like our earthly father would never want us to be sick, the same is true of our Heavenly Father.

In Revelation it's clear that heaven reflects God's will, and that there is no sickness there. Jesus, who is the manifest presence of God (Hebrews 1:3) and revelation of His will, healed the sick and also prayed that the Father's will be done on earth as it is in heaven (Matthew 6:10).

We tend to dwell on the negatives of our battles, like why didn't God bring victory in a situation. After all, we know He can. However, the truth is these failures are because He uses us, imperfect beings. What we don't realize is that our experiencing of loss is one of the side effects of the awesome blessing of the fact that he chooses us to bring victory and fight the battle through us. If it was just God and the enemy, there would be no contest, but God chooses to use the lower creature (humans) to bring victory for His greater glory. He does that through us, which is an awesome blessing. However, because we play a part in this battle, there will be failures. We are, as Paul puts it in 1 Corinthians 3:9, co-workers in God's service. We, of course, play a much lesser role, but we do play one.

An example of this can be seen in Judges 20 when the Israelites go to fight the Benjamites. There were two times that Israel asked God if they should go fight the Benjamites, and God said yes. Yet, both times they were defeated. In fact, they lost thousands of men. They asked God, and God said yes. So, it was God's will for them to fight, but yet they lost both times. See even though they asked God if they should go, they went without proper preparation. Then they asked a third time, and again God said yes. However, this time they fasted and offered burnt sacrifices, and when they went out, they had victory this time. They asked each time, but it wasn't until they did their own preparation through sacrifices and offerings that they had the victory.

Likewise, when the disciples couldn't cast the demon out of the boy in Mark 9, they asked Jesus why they failed. He said, "This kind can come out by nothing but prayer and fasting." In other words, this kind you will only defeat after you properly prepare yourselves spiritually.

So, while God could just choose to wipe out the enemy all the time by Himself, He chooses to use the church instead. So, the failure is not because He's choosing that outcome. The fact is we are in a real battle that is a bit more complicated than that.

While we do play a part, the victory is always God's. So what is our part? Our part is obedience, which is to prepare and to go. Our success in God's eyes is that we prepare and go. The results are up to Him.

In preparation what we are doing is aligning our hearts with God's, renewing our minds, and preparing a place for God's grace to rest. When we fast, for example, we aren't earning something. Rather we are emptying ourselves of the things of this world to allow for more of God in our lives. This allows for greater grace.

Any ability we get is purely by God's grace. Again, it's not something we have earned. So, when we use those abilities, we are blessed in that we are used. However, the victory still belongs to God.

A perfect example of this is found in 2 Samuel 17 when Absalom asks Hushai for advice as to whether to go to battle against David. Hushai tells Absalom that even he who is valiant, whose heart is like the heart of a lion, will melt completely. The reason being that David is a mighty man, and those who are with him are valiant men. That gives quite a picture of how mighty they were – even men of valor with hearts like lions feared them. Yet, we see David say where they get their strength from in 2 Samuel 22. It's from God.

One of the mighty men, Shammah, stationed himself in the middle of a field and single-handedly took on a whole troop of Philistines (2 Samuel 23:11, 12). Yet, what the Bible says is that the Lord brought about a great victory. That's because, after all, who is it that made him mighty, but God. Likewise, even when we are made powerful to go against the enemy, it's such a blessing, but the victory and all the glory is the Lord's.

We Serve a Good God

Other religions believe that their gods give them sickness to teach them a lesson. Many Christians have adopted this thinking. That's not Biblical. In fact, not only is it wrong teaching, it is demonically inspired. Demonic gods desire to see people suffer, but this is not true of the only true God. For example, we see this in 1 Kings 18 when the prophets of Baal are challenged by Elijah. They thought by cutting themselves they could motivate their god to bring fire. Satan and his demons desire to destroy even those that partner with him. God, on the other hand, has sent His son, Jesus, to allow for those that follow Him to have an abundant life that manifests the fruit of the spirit which include love, joy, and peace. That doesn't mean Christians won't suffer. After all, Jesus said to pick up our cross and follow Him. But we need to realize the source of those afflictions and trials are from the enemy.

The famous football coach, Vince Lombardi, wanted to start back at the basics with his team in training camp. With football in hand, he said, "Gentleman, this is a football." As Christians we sometimes need to get back to the very basics. So, with Bible in hand, I would like to say to all Christians that God is good; He desires good things for you; and He is the source of good things. The devil is bad; he desires bad things for you; and he is the source of bad things. We need to get this. Not just in our brains, but in our hearts because the implications are huge.

If our view of God is distorted, we won't sense His love. In turn, our capacity to accept God's love becomes hindered, which will limit our ability to pass it along. We can't give away something we don't have. That, my friend, is a very good strategy of the devil.

There was a quiz that circulated years ago that asked the following: What is: more evil than the devil, greater than God, poor people have it, rich people need it? I heard that a college class was asked this and thought about the answer for almost an hour before they got the answer. Yet, kindergarteners quickly gave the correct answer – the answer being nothing. Sometimes as we get older we over analyze things, don't we? But Jesus said, "Unless you become like a child, you can't enter the kingdom of God." What is so special about a child? They believe first and understand later. We adults, on the other hand, want to understand before we believe, but that takes away much of the reason for faith. We need to get back to believing in our heart. When I was little, we used the expression accepting Jesus into our heart. It wasn't accepting Jesus into our heads.

> Ephesians 3:17-19 (NIV)
> … so that Christ may **dwell in your hearts through faith**. And I pray that you, being rooted and established in love, may have power, together with all the Lord's holy people, to grasp how wide and long and high and deep is the love of Christ, and **to know this love that surpasses knowledge** – that you may be filled to measure of all the fullness of God.

As the verse above states, Christ dwells in our hearts through faith. As we get older we want proof. We need to see it with our own eyes. Too often we are like Thomas who doubted. He wanted proof.

> John 20:24-25 (NIV)
> Now Thomas (also known as Didymus), one of the Twelve, was not with the disciples when Jesus came. So the other

disciples told him, "We have seen the Lord!" But he said to them, **"Unless I see the nail marks in his hands and put my finger where the nails were, and put my hand into his side, I will not believe."**

The old saying we often hear is, "Seeing is believing." However, what God really values is faith. Once we see, there really isn't the need for faith. What God really admires are those who believe without seeing, those who don't need all the answers.

John 20:26-29 (NIV)
A week later his disciples were in the house again, and Thomas was with them. Though the doors were locked, Jesus came and stood among them and said, "Peace be with you!" Then he said to Thomas, "Put your finger here; see my hands. Reach out your hand and put it into my side. Stop doubting and believe."
Thomas said to him, "My Lord and my God!" Then Jesus told him, **"Because you have seen me, you have believed; blessed are those who have not seen and yet have believed."**

Since we are spiritual as well as physical, there are some things we know in our spirit by revelation of the Holy Spirit, that we can't really logically explain. At least it will sometimes take a period of time for our heads to catch up with our heart. I think that's what Paul is referring to when he refers to something called the eyes of our heart. Our hearts can sometimes take things in that our heads just aren't ready for yet.

Ephesians 1:18, 19 (NIV)
I pray that the **eyes of your heart may be enlightened** in order **that you may know** the hope to which he has called you, the riches of his glorious inheritance in his holy people, and his comparably great power for us who believe…

The verses above say that you may know. Yet, Paul is not referring to knowing in our heads. I'm not saying throw your brains out. I'm just saying there will be things in our lives that don't make sense to us. In those times go to what you know and hang on to them. God is good. God loves you. God is for you.

The Manifest Revelation of God's Compassion

One of my favorite inspirational movies is <u>Rudy</u>. In that movie a priest says to Rudy, "Son, in thirty-five years of religious study, I've come up with only two hard, incontrovertible facts: there is a God, and, I'm not Him."

One of the things I have learned to say in praying for the sick is "I don't know." Sometimes we just don't know why things happen and why things don't happen. However, a couple of things I do know are 1) all that came to Jesus for healing got healed, and 2) I'm not Jesus.

So, rather than wrestle with what is and isn't God's will, let's just realize that we aren't God. But, if we really want to see God's will, look at Jesus.

Jesus said in John 14 that if you have seen Me, you have seen the Father. Jesus is a perfect image of God the Father.

> Hebrews 1: 1-2 (NIV)
> In the past God spoke to our ancestors through the prophets at many times and in various ways, **but in these last days He has spoken to us by His Son**, whom He appointed heir of all things, and through whom also He made the universe.

Now make careful note of verse 3.

Hebrews 1: 3 (NIV)
The Son is the radiance of God's glory and the exact representation of His being...

Jesus was the manifest revelation of the Father's heart, and we need to realize that people were constantly drawn to Jesus because of His love and compassion.

I think one of the places that shows His compassion best is in the shortest verse in the Bible, "Jesus wept." When Lazarus died, Jesus wept. Even though He knew He was going to raise him from the dead. Why? It was His compassion for Mary and Martha. What that tells me is that when we lose a loved one, His heart breaks with ours. He is present with those grieving while saying goodbye to their loved one even though they go to be with God and He knows they are ok. He's partaking in the celebration of another believer who just arrived home at the same time. He's God, He can do that. He can be more than one place while simultaneously feeling different emotions at those different locations. However, my point is that He cares more than we can imagine when we suffer loss.

Jesus was seen to have compassion throughout the gospels. Below are a few examples:

He showed compassion to the weary.

Matthew 9:36
But when He saw the multitudes **He was moved with compassion** for them, because they were weary and scattered like sheep without a shepherd.

He showed compassion to those in need.

Mark 8:2
"I have compassion on the multitude because they have continued with me for three days and have nothing to eat."

He often healed out of compassion.

Matthew 14:14
And when Jesus went out He saw a great multitude; and **He was moved with compassion** for them, and healed their sick.

Matthew 20:34
So Jesus had compassion and touched their eyes. And immediately their eyes received sight, and they followed Him.

Mark 1:41
Then **Jesus, moved with compassion**, stretched out His hand and touched him, and said to him, "I am willing; be cleansed."

Luke 7:12, 13
And when He came near the gate of the city, behold, a dead man was being carried out, the only son of his mother; and she was a widow. And a large crowd from the city was with her. When the Lord saw her, **He had compassion** on her and said to her, "Do not weep."

He told stories of compassion.

Luke 10:33
But a certain Samaritan, as he journeyed, came where he was: and when he saw him, **he was moved with compassion,**

Luke 15:20 (NIV)
So he got up and went to his father. But while he was still a long way off, his father saw him and **was filled with compassion** for him; he ran to his son, threw his arms around him and kissed him.

Are you getting the picture of how big a deal compassion is to God? Not sympathy, but compassion because it has action associate with it.

Now to have the proper ministry, one that looks like Jesus, we need two things: compassion and power.

The compassion of God needs to flow though us, but it all comes out of a deep relationship with God. It's all about a relationship with God. That's where we learn the Father's heart. That's where we and God get in sync. It's a partnership, and with that we aren't just doing what we are told or doing because we are told, but rather we share the common desires.

John 15:15
No longer do I call you servants, for a servant does not know what his master is doing; but I have called you friends…

So, we need to spend time getting to know Him. We need to spend time getting to know His heart so it grows in ours. Our heart and His heart need to become aligned, and that all starts at the secret place. That is where we and God get some alone time.

Personally, I love to see miracles, especially miracles of healing. Why? I love to see God's glory, and I love seeing God tell someone He loves them tangibly.

When someone is healed, delivered, or even better, accepts Christ, my favorite thing to see is tears of joy when they realize God loves them in a personal way.

One time we were eating frozen yogurt with some friends and sharing testimonies. One of girls at the table was suddenly showing a lot of pain in her mouth due to having wisdom teeth pulled. My wife, Risa, reached over and said a simple prayer. It couldn't have been more than a five second prayer. The next thing I saw was the girl open her mouth real big. Her eyes got real big, like she was in shock. Then tears started coming down her face when she realized that God just touched her and took all her pain away. It's one thing to know God loves you in your head. However, to experience it takes it to a whole new level.

Seeing Through God's Eyes

The first thing to have an effective ministry is we need to have God's heart for people. To start with, I want to see people the way God sees them. There is a lady that's a friend of my wife who always seems to know how to pray for people, even people she has never met. I asked her how she knows how to pray, and she said it all started when she asked God to allow her to see people the way He sees them. With God's help, we will not only have others' needs revealed, we will see how precious and valuable they are to God.

One time my city was doing a day of outreach to those in need. We provided maps to churches that were participating in the event, where people could get food, clothing, and services (including haircuts, financial help, car repair, bicycle repair, etc.). Those participating would register and get a map in one church where we gave them instructions and also offered prayer to them. During the event, a lady who was a prostitute came into the church. She felt extremely uncomfortable. Yet, at the same time she felt drawn to the presence that she felt there. The conflict was obvious. We had the opportunity to share the gospel and pray with her. She was very excited about the fact that Jesus offered her a new life; He offered her a fresh new start.

See, while some may see her as not that significant to the kingdom, God sees her as a princess. And that is part of what we prayed. That she would see herself as God saw her, a beautiful new creation in Christ. She needed to know that she was so valuable in God's eyes that He sent His only Son to die for her.

Beyond the heart, the mind is to be aligned as well. If we are to work from the position of one kingdom to impact the other, we need to change how we think.

That's why the Bible says we need our minds renewed.

> Romans 12:2
> And do not be conformed to this world, but be transformed by the renewing of your mind, that you may prove what is that good and acceptable and perfect will of God.

The goal is to become familiar with God, not just His acts or deeds. It's about knowing Him. It's about getting to know Him more and more. That's how your mind is renewed. As you get closer to God, you develop more of the mind of Christ.

> 1 Corinthians 2:15, 16
> But he who is spiritual judges all things, yet he himself is rightly judged by no one. For "who has known the mind of the Lord that he may instruct Him?" **But we have the mind of Christ.**

According to Romans 12:2 the transformation by the renewing of your mind is so that you may prove what is that acceptable and perfect will of God. So, how do we do that? It's by practice in everyday life.

The implication is that you can't prove (or show this) without the transformation of your mind.

In Mark 8: 14-16, Jesus is teaching His disciples something about the influence of the political and religious spirit, but they think He's concerned about whether they packed lunch. Then in verse 17 He says, "Are your hearts hard?" They may think, "What did I do wrong? I did everything you said. I'm a good worker. I put my time in." That's exactly how a performance-based Christian thinks. It's also how a legalistic Christian thinks. It's not so much about what we do as to why we do it. It's a heart issue.

Jesus said, "Do you not see and understand?" See, your heart affects whether you can see and hear. We see this very clearly in Isaiah 6, spoken of them whose hearts are unreceptive.

> Isaiah 6:9-10
> And He said, "Go, and tell this people:
> 'Keep on hearing, but do not understand;
> Keep on seeing, but do not perceive.'
> "Make the heart of this people dull,
> And their ears heavy,
> And shut their eyes;
> Lest they see with their eyes,
> And hear with their ears,
> And understand with their heart,
> And return and be healed.

Your heart condition will affect the capability to see spiritually. Seek Him, and He will reveal Himself to you. It's partially that God wants to be pursued. It's also partially that the right heart is one that can be trusted.

No one ever earns the ability to be trusted by works that they do. They earn the ability to be trusted by the relationship they have cultivated. That relationship has an impact on your heart. The heart's condition and relationship go hand in hand. God took that first step in the relationship. The Bible says we love because He first loved us. The question is how do we respond to that expression of love? Jesus didn't die for us just to have us do work. He did it primarily to have relationship.

Also, remember grace precedes works.

Ephesians 2:8-10 (NIV)
For it is by grace you have been saved, through faith—and this is not from yourselves, it is the gift of God— not by works, so that no one can boast. For we are God's handiwork, created in Christ Jesus to do good works, which God prepared in advance for us to do.

It's by grace that we are saved and enter the Christian life, and it's only by God's grace that we can live the Christian life. That goes for what we can accomplish for Him as well as living a holy life.

The Power of
the Testimony

Part of the renewing of the mind is also achieved by remembering.

> Mark 8:18-20
> Having eyes, do you not see? And having ears, do you not hear? And do you not remember? When I broke the five loaves for the five thousand, how many baskets full of fragments did you take up?"
> They said to Him, "Twelve."
> "Also, when I broke the seven for the four thousand, how many large baskets full of fragments did you take up?"
> And they said, "Seven."

The disciples could recall the details of feeding the four thousand, but they totally missed the point.

> Mark 8: 21
> So He said to them, "How is it you do not understand?"

They remembered, but they didn't get it. They could remember the details of the situation, but it didn't have an impact on how they were to think. Jesus says, "How is it you do not understand?"

When you see or experience what many like to call a "God thing," those aren't just memories to be added in your memory bank. They are to have an impact on how you now see things. It's part of the process of renewing of the mind and changing your vision. That is the power of a testimony. God's personal record in your life changes the way you think, and it helps your faith grow.

One time I was to preach at the local jail the next day, and I had lost my voice. With what little voice I had left, I called my team to remind them of our service the next morning. As I spoke to one of my team members, I asked him to keep me in his prayers since I was to preach the next morning. Well, he prayed with me right there on the phone, and when he prayed it felt like a cold wind rushed down my throat. I got my voice back, and my throat was almost completely healed in seconds. I think it would have gotten totally healed right there on the phone if it wasn't for my complete shock of what was happening. This was my first encounter with a healing through which all of my new paradigm of divine healing would be birthed.

A year or more later, I was teaching on the book of James, and I meditated on the passage in chapter five that I was to teach on the next week. It was the verses where it says that Elijah had a nature like ours and the verses on asking for the elders to pray for you if you were sick. At the time, I needed surgery for my rotator cuff. It was torn, and I could hardly lift my arm at all. I would like to state here that I never like to teach anything I don't fully believe. That being the case, I struggled with Elijah and I having a similar nature. He did so many miracles, and I never experienced any from my prayers. So, I prayed about this struggle. Then I next prayed about who to have pray for my shoulder since I was also to teach on the passage about having the elders pray for the sick. I wanted to practice what I taught, but we had no elders in our church at the time. Then I remembered the healing of my throat and wondered if I should have the same man who prayed with me then pray for my shoulder. Well, apparently the power of the testimony was enough because right after that I noticed I could lift my arm when I went to put my Bible on the desk. In fact, I got my wife out of bed and had her throw a softball with me in the street. For the first time in years, I could throw without pain. This was all the result of remembering a testimony.

As I mentioned, I was teaching on James when I had the torn rotator cuff, but at the time I didn't think to consider it joy. But God said to me during that time, "I will make you lie down in green pastures." I had a huge peace come on me because of that even though I didn't know what He meant by it at the time. Now, in hind sight, I wouldn't trade my torn rotator cuff for a $1,000,000. This is not an exaggeration. As I said, in the midst of it, God said to me, "I will make you lie down in green pastures."

Jesus revealed a ministry to me that I never saw possible, one of healing and deliverance. That is casting out demons and praying for miracles of healing.

It's the work of the Holy Spirit in a manner that I had never seen before. One I knew existed, but thought only accessible to a special few. My eyes have now been opened.

We want to get to the point where we have eyes that see and ears that hear. That is, we want spiritual eyes and spiritual ears. So, you can see what God is doing, and you can hear what God is saying. My prayer for the church is the words spoken in Isaiah 29:18.

Isaiah 29:18 (NIV)
In that day the deaf will hear the words of the scroll, and out of gloom and darkness the eyes of the blind will see.

However, when you can't see and can't hear, we, at least, should remember the things we have seen God do. That is the power of a testimony. That's a large part of what makes a testimony so powerful. It builds faith, and it helps change how we see.

The healing I received that helped set me on my quest to know more about healing actually occurred with no one praying. It occurred when I had remembered receiving healing in my throat when someone prayed for me.

Remembering that healing of my throat brought faith. That faith then brought healing without anyone even praying. This is one of the reasons it's very important to keep a log of testimonies, to remember when God showed up in a personal way.

This is why the Israelites put up monuments and celebrated past events like Passover. It's important to remember the acts of God because they should impact how we live. When it comes to healing, it's even more powerful when there has been a testimony of the exact same issue that you are faced with (cancer, broken marriage, an addiction).

As I mentioned earlier, the Bible says Jesus was moved with compassion and healed all that came to Him. We can know truth like that, but there is something about the personal testimony that really builds faith.

Now, there is a dangerous side of the testimony, as well as helpful. Like anything that has power, it needs to be properly used, or it can be dangerous. For example, if I just saw three people healed of whatever, let's pick scoliosis, and I share the testimonies with the next person I'm going to pray for, what happens if they don't get healed? Right away they think, "What's wrong with me?" This doesn't mean you don't work to build their faith with the testimonies, but you need to be very sensitive to the fact that Satan can throw that back in their face if they don't get healed. The thing to keep in mind is that the person is the priority, not the healing. The fact is there may be many reasons why they might not have received healing; many of which are not their fault. So, you need to be sensitive, and make sure they don't believe any lies of the enemy of unworthiness or that God doesn't love them. This is where you need to be sensitive to the Holy

Spirit. For example, there may be a bigger issue going on than the physical problem that God wants to heal, but that doesn't mean God doesn't want to bring physical healing as well. God is first and foremost concerned about a person's spirit, next his soul, and lastly his body. However, He does care about all three. If He didn't care about the body, He wouldn't make a point of saying it is the temple of the Holy Spirit (1 Corinthians 6:19).

Power is Imparted, but the Holy Spirit is a Person

If we are to live the life that reflects Jesus, we obviously have to live lives of power. It's important to make a quick mention that power doesn't look the same for everyone. Just like the church is made of many members of a variety of gifts, the power seen, and even sometimes not seen (but still present), will be different among the body of believers.

Jesus demonstrated what the Christian life was to look like. Remember when He brought up the issue of the Blasphemy of the Holy Spirit? What was the context? Casting out demons, and I believe doing miracles as well. When Jesus did miracles, it was through the Holy Spirit. He didn't do them in His own power. In fact, I believe this is also why He often referred to Himself as the Son of Man. To show us what we could potentially do through the work of the Holy Spirit. We are Christians. Christ means anointed one. The Spirit of God came on Jesus when He was baptized. He then started His ministry and did His first miracles.

The Holy Spirit was on Jesus without limit. Paul says to us in Ephesians 5:18 to be filled with the Holy Spirit. Jesus had no limit.

Now we are Christians, little anointed ones. God did not leave us helpless and powerless to do His work, and He didn't leave us powerless to live the Christian life.

> Acts 1:8 (NIV)
> But you will **receive power** when the Holy Spirit comes on you…

> 1 Corinthians 2:4-5 (NIV)
> My message and my preaching were not with wise and persuasive words, but with a **demonstration of the Spirit's power**, so that your faith might not rest on human wisdom, but on God's power.

> 1 Corinthians 4:20 (NIV)
> For the kingdom of God is not a matter of talk **but of power**.

My dad got me involved in jail ministry when I was very young. When I preach at jail, I want people at jail to know that God has the power to transform their lives. It's not about religion. It's about a relationship with a powerful God who loves us.

One time my older son, two others, and I were ministering at the jail. I normally have more help, but we were shorthanded that morning. So, we split into two teams of two. My son and I were one team, and he was to preach. We had no worship leader, but I had some song books. I did my best to try to lead us in singing, but it was terrible. The inmates were not at all engaging in the singing, and I was out of my comfort zone in leading worship to start with. It was miserable. I felt they all wished they could just leave, as did I. So, I quickly transitioned to prayer time. I asked if anyone had any prayer requests, and they all were unresponsive. They just stared at me with dead stares. Well, I noticed when they walked in that someone had walked in with a limp. So, I asked him what was going on with his leg. He said he hurt it, but other than that I can't remember the details other than it was painful for him. So, I said, "Well, let's start with you," and I prayed for his leg. We aren't allowed to touch the inmates, so I kept my hand about an inch away from the point of injury. I could feel power coming off of my hand. I asked him to check it out, and he said it felt better. I said, "Praise God, let's pray some more." He then said it felt 100%. I then heard someone speak something in Spanish to the guy next to him, and I asked what he said. He said he couldn't believe what I just did. To which I responded, "It's not me who healed, but God in me. This is why we have come, to tell you of a God who is real, is powerful, and can help you live the life you should live. So, who else would like prayer for something?" This was a turning point for the service because almost every hand went up. Most importantly, it opened them up to the gospel as my son preached. People don't want religion. They need to know of a God who loves them, wants a relationship with them, and wants to transform their lives.

People are looking for something real. If we offer them just religion, they will go elsewhere to try and fill their needs. Again this is where there is power in a testimony. The biggest testimony one can share is that of a transformed life. Regardless of what the testimony is, however, there needs to be something they can see, or even better something they can experience. Jesus modeled this for us throughout the gospels. Sometimes it was a healing. Sometimes it was a supernatural word of knowledge such as with the lady at the well.

While we can tend to think of power associated with the Holy Spirit, He is not a power or a force. I remember one time I was in my car thinking about outreach. I thought of how equipped I was and the tools that I had on my evangelistic belt. I had the word of God, sharper than any two edged sword; I had my evangelistic message; and I had the power of the Holy Spirit. Then I felt one of the biggest rebukes from the Holy Spirit ever. I really felt Him say to me, "I'm not a Power. I am a person." Then I'm not sure if the next thought was His or mine, but I felt him say, "If anything you are a tool on my belt."

I quickly repented and apologized. Then I said to him, "Please, make me one of your favorite tools."

It was just a reminder to me of how often we get things mixed up in our thinking. One of the most confusing things about the Holy Spirit is terminology.

- Baptism of the Holy Spirit.
- Filled with the Holy Spirit.
- Indwelt with the Holy Spirit.
- The anointing of the Holy Spirit.
- The presence of the Holy Spirit.
- The falling of the Holy Spirit on a person or group of people.

So, while I'll attempt to help with this, I really don't want terminology to be a barrier for what I'm attempting to explain.

I want to start by distinguishing between the work of the Holy Spirit baptizing us into the body of Christ when we become saved and being baptized with the Holy Spirit. The first one is an act that the Holy Spirit does for us. The second one is something Jesus does.

When people get saved, they have the Holy Spirit reside in them to teach them and help them live a Holy life. We use the term, "indwelt with the Holy Spirit" to describe this.

Romans 8:9 (NIV)
You, however, are not in the realm of the flesh but are in the realm of the Spirit, if indeed the Spirit of God lives in you. And if anyone does not have the Spirit of Christ, they do not belong to Christ.

The above verse speaks of the indwelling of the Holy Spirit, which all believers have.

When a person becomes saved, that is he realizes he is a sinner and destined for hell, but he has placed his faith in Jesus' death and shed blood on the cross as payment for his sins, the Holy Spirit comes into his life. When this happens, that person's spirit is transformed, and he becomes a new creature. This is such a radical transformation, that Jesus says that this person has been born again.

John 3:5-6 (NIV)
Jesus answered, "Very truly I tell you, no one can enter the kingdom of God unless they are born of water and the Spirit. Flesh gives birth to flesh, but the Spirit gives birth to spirit."

When a person is born of the Spirit, he can enter heaven. At that point he is saved, and he is indwelled by the Spirit of God. The indwelling of the Holy Spirit will produce the fruit of the Spirit in that person's life. These are listed in Galatians 5:22-23 to be love, joy, peace, forbearance, kindness, goodness, faithfulness, gentleness, and self-control.

So, when was Jesus born in the Spirit? He was born of both, flesh and the Spirit, when He was born on earth.

Matthew 1:20 (NIV)
But after he had considered this, an angel of the Lord appeared to him in a dream and said, "Joseph son of David, do not be afraid to take Mary home as your wife, because what is conceived in her is from the Holy Spirit.

Luke 1:35 (NIV)
The angel answered, "The Holy Spirit will come on you, and the power of the Most High will overshadow you. So, the holy one to be born will be called the Son of God.

Since Jesus was born of the Spirit at birth, it makes sense that the Holy Spirit indwelt Him from the beginning of taking on the form of man. The Holy Spirit taught Him and created the fruit of the Spirit in

His life. This is why it says in Luke 2 that Jesus could amaze scholars in the temple at just twelve years old.

However, at the age of thirty, we see the Holy Spirit come down on Jesus. This is what we refer to as the baptism of the Holy Spirit or filling of the Holy Spirit. It is the baptism of the Holy Spirit that equips, or empowers, one for ministry. In Jesus' case it coincided with His water baptism. However, that is not usually that case with most Christians. The other uniqueness of the Baptism of the Holy Spirit for Jesus was that it was a one-time occurrence. For many believers, there are multiple baptisms of the Holy Spirit, at which something more is given at each event.

Being filled with the Holy Spirit, the Baptism of the Holy Spirit, or the Baptism with the Holy Spirit are different terms for the same thing. However, I don't want to spend time discussing terminology as much as the purpose. The purpose of the filling of the Holy Spirit or Holy Spirit baptism is to equip us for ministry. Often times when we see this happen in the Bible it says the Spirit fell on people. This provides a picture that I think is very helpful to distinguish between the indwelling of the Holy Spirit and the Baptism of the Holy Spirit. When we are saved, the Holy Spirit comes in us (indwelling) to teach us and help us live lives that produce the fruit of the Spirit. When we receive the Baptism of the Holy Spirit, the Holy Spirit is on us, and He equips us for ministry. Again, the Holy Spirit is in us for us, and on us to empower us to minister to others.

In Matthew 3:11, Mark 1:8, Luke 3:16, and John 1:33 John the Baptist used the term Baptism since that's what he was doing.

John the Baptist said Jesus would baptize us with the Holy Spirit.

Now the important connection. Acts 1:5-8 says you will be baptized with the Holy Spirit and will receive power. This is speaking of what? This is speaking of Pentecost.

So, let me ask you a question. When did the disciples (the 11) receive (become indwelled with) the Holy Spirit?

> John 20:20-23 (NIV)
> After He said this, He showed them His hands and side. The disciples were overjoyed when they saw the Lord. Again Jesus said. "Peace be with you! As the Father has sent Me, I am sending you." **And with that He breathed on them and said, "Receive the Holy Spirit.** If you forgive anyone's sins, their sins are forgiven; if you do not forgive them, they are not forgiven."

Here we saw the eleven disciples received the Holy Spirit prior to Pentecost. That is, they became indwelled with the Holy Spirit in John 20.

However, they became filled or baptized with the Holy Spirit at Pentecost.

> Acts 2:4 (NIV)
> All of them were **filled** with the Holy Spirit and began to speak in tongues as the Spirit enabled them.

> Acts 2:16-21 (NIV)
> … this is what was spoken by the prophet Joel: 'In the last days, God says, I will pour out my Spirit on all people. Your sons and daughters will prophesy, your young men will see visions, your old men will dream dreams. Even on my servants, both men and women, I will pour out my Spirit in those days, and they will prophesy. I will show wonders in the heavens above and signs on the earth below, blood and fire and billows of smoke. The sun will be turned to darkness and the moon to blood before the coming of the great and glorious day of the Lord. And everyone who calls on the name of the Lord will be saved.'

It's interesting that Joel says nothing about speaking in tongues, and most of the things in Joel weren't originally seen at Pentecost. Yet, Peter says that this passage was being fulfilled. The point is that these types of things would happen. So, let's be careful not to put God in a box. In fact, speaking in tongues is not the only possible evidence of being filled with the Holy Spirit. Even Paul said in 1Cor 12:30, "Do all speak in tongues?"

So, how does one get filled with the Spirit? Well, as Jesus suggests, they should ask for it.

> Luke 11:11-13 (NIV)
> "Which of you fathers, if your son asks for a fish, will give him a snake instead? Or if he asks for an egg, will give him a scorpion? If you then, though you are evil, know how to give good gifts to your children, how much more will your Father in heaven **give the Holy Spirit to those who ask Him!**"

It's interesting that Jesus discusses asking for something we tend to think is automatic upon becoming a Christian, but here we are talking about the filling of the Holy Spirit, not the indwelling of the Holy Spirit. Again, if the filling were automatic, as the indwelling is, there would be no need to ask the Father for it to happen.

Also, as James says when you ask for something from God (wisdom in the context of James), you should do so with expectation (faith).

> James 1:6 (NIV)
> But when you ask, you must believe and not doubt, because the one who doubts is like a wave of the sea, blown and tossed by the wind.

Of course, we often see the filling come through impartation through the laying on of hands such as in Acts 8:14-17.

Acts 8:14-17 (NIV)
When the apostles in Jerusalem heard that Samaria had accepted the word of God, they sent Peter and John to Samaria. When they arrived, they prayed for the new believers there that they might receive the Holy Spirit, because the Holy Spirit had not yet come on any of them; they had simply been baptized in the name of the Lord Jesus. Then Peter and John **placed their hands on them**, and they received the Holy Spirit.

Paul tells Timothy not to neglect the gift imparted to him through the laying on of hands.

1 Timothy 4:14 (NIV)
Do not neglect your gift, which was given you through prophecy when the body of elders **laid their hands on you**.

With the laying on of hands, there is also often a release of a spiritual gift, or gifts, during the impartation.

Romans 1:11 (NIV)
I long to see you so that I may **impart** to you some **spiritual gift** to make you strong—

That's how it happened for me. When a great man of God laid his hands on me, I didn't feel anything at the time until I started to walk away when he was done, and every bone in my body ached like I had just been electrocuted. It was after that event that I felt power when I prayed and would start to see people healed.

While I believe the easiest way to receive a gift is by having someone moving in that gift lay hands on and pray for one to receive it, there is no control over what the Holy Spirit will decide to do. For example, I've had people receive gifts when I pray for them that

I don't even move in. There is also no control over the amount of impartation that will take place.

What I do know is that the laying on of hands and baptisms are things that were meant to be fundamental to our faith.

> Hebrews 6:1, 2
> Therefore, leaving the discussion of the elementary principles of Christ, let us go on to perfection, not laying again the foundation of repentance from dead works and of faith toward God, of the **doctrine of baptisms**, of **laying on of hands**, of resurrection of the dead, and of eternal judgment.

If we look at Acts, we see that with the filling of the Holy Spirit there is often some visible manifestation. However, there doesn't have to be. And more importantly, it doesn't have to look the same for every person.

> Acts 8:18 (NIV)
> When **Simon saw that the Spirit was given** at the laying on of the apostles' hands, he offered them money

> Acts 19: 1-6 (NIV)
> While Apollos was at Corinth, Paul took the road through the interior and arrived at Ephesus. There he found some disciples and asked them, "Did you receive the Holy Spirit when you believed?" They answered, "No, we have not even heard that there is a Holy Spirit." So Paul asked, "Then what baptism did you receive?"
> "John's baptism," they replied. Paul said, "John's baptism was a baptism of repentance. He told the people to believe in the one coming after him, that is, in Jesus." On hearing this, they were baptized in the name of the Lord Jesus. When Paul placed his hands on them, the Holy Spirit came on them, and they **spoke in tongues and prophesied**.

It should also be noted that not everyone will be equipped the same.

> 1 Corinthians 12:29-30 (NIV)
> Are all apostles? Are all prophets? Are all teachers? Do all work miracles? Do all have gifts of healing? Do all speak in tongues? Do all interpret?

The sign that you have been baptized with the Holy Spirit (or filled with the Holy Spirit) is that you will have power for ministry. That is power for the ministry that God is calling you to, not for whatever you want to do.

There are great books on this subject. So I won't go into very much depth. The important thing to note is that there is more power to be had for the purpose of ministry. It should also be noted that it's not only a onetime event. There can be multiple fillings or baptisms.

I want to point out here that a person's gifting is never something he has earned or a reflection of how spiritual he is.

However, often the size of your filling depends on how empty you are. As I mentioned earlier, we Americans all tend to be pretty full of the things of this world. As we submit more of those areas to God, there is more room for Him to come in. However, it's more than a yielding to the Holy Spirit, it's "an anointing" to use Old Testament terminology.

I find that this is one of the large benefits of fasting. Many people fast because they want to show God their desire for more. I believe when it comes to the filling of the Holy Spirit, that fasting allows for greater capacity as it helps a person empty himself in the process of the things of this world. There are many other spiritual benefits to fasting, but I wanted to make mention of this relative to the desire for more of the Holy Spirit.

Of course, whenever you go to church or spend personal time with God, you are filled. That's not what I'm talking about. I'm talking about a significant event that has a large impact on you spiritually, and it supernaturally empowers gifting in you for ministry God has for you to do. Of course, going to church, spending time in worship, and all the spiritual disciplines are important in order to keep ourselves filled.

Now that begs the question, how can you have more of a person? While the Holy Spirit is a person, and as we know God is everywhere, there is an attribute of God's presence that is hard to understand. We see this in the very fact that Paul could get the presence of God onto a handkerchief that would then carry the power to heal (Acts 19:12).

It might be helpful to go back to the phrase anointed with Holy Spirit. Anointed means to smear or rub on with. When we look at this definition it might be easier to understand. Christians have the Holy Spirit in them (indwelt) for themselves. However, Christians get anointed with the Holy Spirit for others. That is, the Holy Spirit is on them for others. And the amount of the Holy Spirit on them, or the amount of their anointing, will vary. The anointing and their gifting will align with their calling.

It's important to note that a person can be talented and articulate and not be anointed by God to teach. Likewise, someone may have a talent or ability to present the gospel very clearly, but not be anointed as an evangelist. Also, a person may be a very talented musician and not have an anointing as a worship leader. The anointing and gifting that comes from God is supernatural. It's something that's not necessarily obvious to the human eye other than the amazing results that come when using that supernatural gifting. Yet, it can often be tangible. We can often feel the effects of an anointed person using their gift. This may come in all kinds of forms depending on the persons gifting. For example it can be electricity, heat, healing, conviction, joy, or peace just to name a few.

The Presence of God and the Power of Worship

There is power in the presence of God, or one could say the presence of God is what brings power. This is something that can't be explained as easily until you have experienced it. We tend to think God is everywhere. While that is theologically possible, it's at minimum abstract. When I say God is more present in one place than another, that may seem abstract as well, but it's tangible too. In a dream Jacob saw angels ascending and descending, and he said, "God is in this place." Even though this was in a dream, the presence of God was tangible. He saw it, and he heard God. There are times when you can feel the presence of evil. It's tangible. Likewise, there are times you can feel a strong presence of God. It's tangible, and it's awesome.

In those places and times when I have been in the strong presence of God, my spiritual gifts are greatly magnified. So, what does this mean? Simple, with the presence of God comes power. Because there is power in the presence of God, it also empowers my gifts, such as my gift of healing. It's like the gifts are power tools, but without being hooked up to the power source, they can't do anything.

In the case of healing, God's presence makes all the difference. It's even mentioned in Jesus ministry in Luke 5:17.

Luke 5:17 (NIV)
One day Jesus was teaching, and Pharisees and teachers of the law were sitting there. They had come from every village of Galilee and from Judea and Jerusalem. **And the power of the Lord was with Jesus to heal the sick.**

The "power of the Lord" spoken of in this verse is the presence of the Holy Spirit. I find it interesting that this was explicitly stated because the Spirit of God followed Jesus everywhere He went, as well as an open heaven (John 1:51).

My wife and I used to head up a healing ministry, and we have a place called a healing room where people can come for prayer. One night we experienced a healing momentum in our ministry where the presence of God became so strong a couple of people got healed just by walking through the door of the healing room.

Furthermore, the times that I have seen the greatest acts of healing as a result of my own prayers are when I have been at a conference where the presence of the Holy Spirit is unmistakably strong. So, what about these conferences is it that makes the presence so strong? Two things come to mind. One is the presence of very spiritually anointed people. The second, and more important one, is a group of people who really worship. I don't know how to explain this. You need to experience it. There were times when I have been in a place where the worship is so strong, I honestly didn't know worship like that existed. One time I was at a service at a church that my wife and I had traveled to visit. The worship was so strong that when the speaker finally went up after hours of intense worship, a lady immediately went up to the stage because she couldn't wait any longer. She wanted to know what she needed to do to be saved.

54

When we enter into worship, it not only affects us, it affects our whole environment including those around us. Remember Paul and Silas in Acts 16? They were in jail and chained. What did they do? They prayed, but then what? They sang praises. When they did that, the Bible says an earthquake occurred. Doors opened, and chains broke. This is literally physical in this story, but the same holds true in the spiritual as well. Praise opens spiritual doors, and praise breaks spiritual chains and spiritual bonds. Doors opening and chains breaking is a picture of evangelism and deliverance. Doors or hearts are open. Chains of sin are broken. Praise is powerful!

Now in the story of Paul and Silas in jail, the earthquake happens, and it makes sense that could have opened the doors. However, chains were loosed, and that doesn't occur from an earthquake. What is my point? In the story it wasn't just Paul's and Silas's chains that opened, but everyone's. Their praise had an effect on their whole environment, and that wasn't just an accident. And what was the result of it all? People got saved! So, it's a picture of how we create an atmosphere for those to come into the kingdom.

Besides prayer, worship is probably the most underestimated power in this world. In the spiritual realm, worship is like an act of violence. It's powerful. A friend of mine told me a story of a guy calling his church because his wife was manifesting a demon. The pastor called my friend for help, and together they tried laboriously to cast out the demon. They did everything to command this demon to go, but it wouldn't. So, they decided to worship. As they stood there and sang praises to God, the demon couldn't handle it, and it left. A great peace came over the woman, and she ended up giving her life to the Lord.

To be open and honest, I used to be at a place where I would be okay if we just skipped the worship and went straight to the sermon. I just was there to learn something. I didn't understand the power of worshiping with music, and I didn't enjoy it. Now I am often disappointed when it ends. It's enjoyable, empowering, and it's a place I can give something to the Lord. If we are to be proper stewards of this life, a large part of our Christian life needs to be filled with worship. God deserves it.

As I look at the life of David, who was described in the Bible as a man after God's own heart, I also see that he was a mighty warrior. To be a mighty warrior, you need to have courage. David's source of courage was his relationship with the Lord. And that relationship was forged out of worship and meditation on God's Word. David was a worshiper. He worshiped God with his harp. He wrote psalms of praise to the Lord. We see David referred to as Israel's singer of songs in 2 Samuel 23:1, and in 2 Samuel 6 we see David Dancing before the Lord with all his might.

When David saw Goliath, look at what David says in 1 Samuel 17.

> 1 Samuel 17:26 (NIV)
> … Who is this uncircumcised Philistine that he should defy the armies of the living God?"

How dare this uncircumcised Philistine insult his God whom he loved and worshipped. For David, it wasn't about his own reputation, but rather the God whom he worshiped.

I consider myself a teacher of the Bible, whether it is leading family devotions, leading small group, teaching Sunday School, or preaching at the jail. So, when I read the Bible, I typically have looked at it from one of two perspectives: what is God teaching me, and what I can I learn and pass on. While both of these are good, I was missing something. I would listen to sermons of a variety of preachers throughout the week as well, and I had the same outlook on it. I would come to church with the same approach. What can I learn? That's not all bad - don't get me wrong, but there was something missing, which I didn't realize was so powerful, and that is worship and intimacy with God.

So, I had to ask myself, whether entering in personal devotions or coming to church, why am I going? Am I coming only to learn, or am I coming to meet God? See, when I used to come to church, I would half-heartedly sing my praises. Sometimes not even think about the words I was singing and who I was singing them to. Yes, I would still have a successful ministry and Christian walk, but not really with the power coming out of a really close relationship and a heart of worship like God intended.

So, what does it look like when a person worships or idolizes someone? Well, I can think of no better example than when a kid idolizes an athlete. They want to dress like them, act like them, and talk like them. So, our response to God should naturally be so much more since He is so much more deserving of our worship. The goal is to become more Christ-like from our love and worship. In turn, our lives should naturally have an impact on the world. Anytime you love someone, you can't help but talk about them. Likewise, when you worship someone, you also can't help but talk about Him.

As I mentioned earlier, worship will change an environment, but let me bring it back to an individual basis. James 5:13 says, "Is any among you afflicted? Let him pray. Is any merry? Let him sing psalms. Is any among you afflicted? Let him pray." Usually, if we are afflicted we will pray, at least eventually. Some wait until they have tried every-thing else. Now, I want to focus on the second part of this though. Is any merry? That is, has God blessed you? Are things going well? Let him sing psalms. Now this may seem basic. That's like stating the obvious. Yes, of course. I knew that. Really? In reality, when the storms settle, when things are going smoothly, isn't it easy to just forget about God?

When things are bad, Satan will say, "You don't need this, what good is it to be a Christian?" Trouble may take you from God, but if you really have a relationship with Him, you will most likely turn to Him in times of trouble. However, when things are going well, won't Satan say, "You don't need God." Now again, if you really are saved, you know that's not the case. You know you need God. However, when life is going so well, we can just sort of lose sight of God. When did the Israelites usually fall in the Old Testament? When things were going well.

What does James teach? Just go around and sing? No, James says sing Psalms, sing praises. See, it's one thing to go around whistling a tune of the latest secular pop hit. That's natural. Anyone can do that. It's another to worship God with a song of praise on your lips. What James is saying is supernatural.

Prior to this point, I have used the phrase filled with the Spirit as a significant event that can be interchanged with the phrase baptized with the Holy Spirit. However, there is another filling that is necessary on a regular basis simply because we are leaky vessels. It's like food. We need it on a regular basis. Such is the case with the Word of God and worship to keep us filled up. That's what James is talking about when he says we should be going around with songs on our lips. It's also reemphasized by Paul in Ephesians 5:18, 19.

> Ephesians 5: 18, 19 (NIV)
> Do not get drunk on wine, which leads to debauchery. Instead, be filled with the Spirit, speaking to one another with psalms, hymns, and songs from the Spirit. Sing and make music from your heart to the Lord,

Paul commands us to be filled with Spirit, which is not an automatic thing or he wouldn't command it. When you surround yourself with worship, you become more filled with the Spirit. And when you are filled with the Spirit, you will sing praises. It's a cycle that builds on itself. In this day of technology, there is no reason not to be surrounded with worship music and good sermons all of the time.

If someone has a stressful house, I challenge them to have everyone in the house listen to nothing but Christian praise and worship music for a whole day. These days, there is such a wide variety of Christian music that you will find something for everyone's taste. They will see a difference at the end of that day. The reason they will see a difference is that Christian praise and worship music influences behavior. In the verses above Paul contrasts being drunk with wine with being filled with the Spirit. The reason is that he's using an analogy to point out how the Holy Spirit will have influence on our behavior. As we fill ourselves with more of Him, the fruit of the Spirit becomes more evident.

It has also been my experience that there is another attribute of the Holy Spirit highlighted in worship, His holiness. One time when I was at a Christian men's event called Promise Keepers, I had finished eating my lunch early. So, I walked down to the stage to watch the band play before the next session. While down there I began to worship, and guys on each side of me took my hands and lifted them in praise. There was a whole line of us in front with our hands lifted high worshipping God. I felt a strong presence of God, and I remember one of the songs we sang was Holy, Holy, Holy. It's interesting to me that it was the only specific song I remember. From that day forward, I would often become overwhelmed with emotion whenever I would sing a song with the word holy in it. Worship in the form of spiritual songs is a great way to keep ourselves filled, and when His presence shows up strong, sometimes all you can do is stand or kneel in awe.

First Comes Love

Now, for much of my life, I've had a pretty good relationship with God, and I totally depended on the Holy Spirit in ministry. Yet, there was still something lacking. Well, first of all, as I indicated previously, my relationship used to be almost all academic. It was functional, but the relationship lacked the desire or passion to just spend time with God for the sake of spending time with Him. So, I never really sensed His love even though I knew He loved me in my head. It's like a marriage where a couple keeps the home functional, but they never tell each other they love them, and their time together is pure business. Then their job is to tell others how awesome their marriage is. Yes, they could say their spouse loves them. They could say their spouse does stuff for them. But if one looked at their life, would they see a genuinely healthy relationship?

In the church I grew up, we have a banner on the wall that says three core parts of our mission statement: Loving God, Loving people, Making disciples. The progression is from top downward. You start with the great commandment: Love the Lord your God with all your heart, and with all your soul, and with all your mind. Then the second greatest commandment: Love others as yourself. Then the great commission: Go and make disciples. If we really love God, we will love people, which will lead to making disciples. If you take away the first one, you aren't motivated by love, and then you're working out of duty. Then it becomes a works mentality, and much too often we try to evangelize and make disciples out of duty. When you do that, not only is that not effective, you fall into the trap that the church in Ephesus, mentioned in the book of Revelation, fell into.

> Revelation 2:2-4
> I know **your works, your labor**, your patience, and that you cannot bear those who are evil. And you have tested those who say they are apostles and are not, and have found them liars; and you have persevered and have patience, and **have labored for My name's sake** and have not become weary. **Nevertheless I have this against you, that you have left your first love.**

The church of Ephesus was very dutiful, but what God had against them was that they had no love. To the non-spiritual trained eye, they looked like an awesome church because they were so active. However, Jesus threatens to take away their lamp stand, their lamp stand being their church. Even though they are doing all sorts of good stuff, it could actually be a bad testimony if there is no love. See, it could come off as just being self-righteous. Effective ministry has to come from love and relationship. Genuine love manifests passion.

Do you want to do more for the Kingdom and carry out the great commission? I trust your answer is yes. Well, you need to start with the great commandment. In the natural, children are born out of intimacy. The same is true in God's Kingdom. Our love for God is shown in our love for others.

> John 13:35 (NIV)
> By this everyone will know that you are my disciples, if you love one another.

These types of statements about loving God are not to get us to do works in order to make us look like we love Christ. Even though it is a way of showing love to God by making sure that we do works, it's not to be a works mentality. It's a gauge of our relationship. If we want to be obedient to God's word, for example, it's easiest to focus on developing a close and a more intimate relationship with God, rather than to try and force ourselves to live a life of obedience. The intimate relationship, or our love that is developed in that relationship, will make it easy to live a life of obedience and have fruit in our lives. Too often we get it backwards, and we're trying to force the fruit or trying to force ourselves to live a life that reflects a love that doesn't even necessarily exist.

One thing I have found to be in common among those with great ministry is that they enjoy their relationship with God more than their ministry. They cherish their intimacy with Him.

Too often we spend our quiet time with God with our "to do" list for Him. While there is a place for that, that's not relationship. Think about the kind of time you want to spend with your kids. You don't want to only see them when they want something. As you focus on the kind of intimacy you desire with your own children, that will help you work towards a more fruitful experience in your quiet time with God.

Abiding in Christ is the key. We need to stay connected to the Lord. We need that personal relationship to be our solid foundation. Jesus uses the vine and branches as an illustration in John 15:5, "I am the vine, you are the branches. He that abides in me, and I in him, brings forth much fruit." A branch doesn't strain to produce fruit. It just needs to be connected well. He goes on to say, "for without me you can do nothing." Too many Christians don't get that. I know that by their approach to evangelism. So many times we think with our evangelism methods and brilliant arguments we can persuade people to become Christians. We need to understand that it is no less a miracle when a person gets saved than when a blind man gets his sight back if we prayed for it. It's not the words of our prayer that would bring him sight. It's obviously a miracle. Likewise, it's not our great argument that brings someone to the Lord; it's the Holy Spirit working on their hearts. So, we need to depend on God for ministry. Methods are helpful, but without the Holy Spirit working on the person's heart, it's a fruitless exercise.

Back when I was a kid and they put cool toys in cereal boxes, I got a glow in the dark ball. When placed in light, it soaked it up and then became a source of light in the dark. The more it soaked, the greater it shined. Are you getting the picture? The more we soak in His presence, the more our life will shine and displace the darkness.

Isaiah 60:1, 2
Arise, shine; For your light has come! And the glory of the Lord is risen upon you.
For behold, the darkness shall cover the earth, And deep darkness the people;
But the Lord will arise over you, And His glory will be seen upon you.

It says in Isaiah 60 that His glory will rise upon you, and it will be seen upon you. That glory is something people are attracted to.

As it says in Matthew 5:14, we are light to the world.

Matthew 5:14
"You are the light of the world. A city that is set on a hill cannot be hidden.

Why does Jesus use the illustration of a city on a hill? People who are lost in their journey can see a city on a hill, and the light guides them to a place of safety. So, you are a light that is to guide them. Guide them where? There is only one place that there is real safety – that is salvation. We use the expression "lead them to Christ." As we know, Christ is the only way to heaven.

Again, we are a light source. The more we learn to soak in His presence, the more we will be able to let His glory shine on us.

2 Corinthians 3:18 (NIV)
And we all, who with unveiled faces contemplate the Lord's glory, are being transformed into his image with ever-increasing glory, which comes from the Lord, who is the Spirit.

Authority Delegated

We have discussed the importance of power given to us through the Holy Spirit. We briefly discussed the power and importance of love as well. Another important aspect of living the Christian life is authority. As with any responsibility, it can be frustrating if authority to carry it out has been not been given as well.

Many Christians really struggle with the fact that we have authority. The fact of the matter is that we have authority based on who we are in Christ. Our words can carry a lot of power for good or bad. Way too often we underestimate the power our words have. However, I don't want to digress from my main point, and that is the authority we have in order to carry out the great commission.

> Matthew 28:18-20 (NIV)
> Then Jesus came to them and said, "All authority in heaven and on earth has been given to me. Therefore, go and make disciples of all nations, baptizing them in the name of the Father and of the Son and of the Holy Spirit, and teaching them to obey everything I have commanded you. And surely I am with you always, to the very end of the age."

As ambassadors of Christ, we are delegated authority to represent Him. There is power associated with this authority. This is why the great commission is preceded with the statement by Jesus,

"All authority in heaven and on earth has been given to me." The next word He then says is, "Therefore." So, the fact that Jesus has been given all authority is critical to the ability to carry out the great commission.

As I mentioned in the previous section, there is power in the presence of God. I've had times where I've laid my hand on an affliction and the pain immediately moved because it was an afflicting spirit. If you think that sounds strange, it shouldn't when you realize that according to Acts 19:12 the apostle Paul carried so much of the presence of God that you could take a handkerchief that he touched, and it could bring healing and drive out demons. That's amazing.

However, the presence of God will vary from time to time, at least for your average believer like me. Thankfully, we also carry authority when needed. What does this authority do for us as His ambassadors? Well, one passage that sheds light on this is Luke 10:19.

> Luke 10:19 (NIV)
> "I have given you authority to trample on snakes and scorpions and to overcome all the powers of the enemy; nothing will harm you."

In that verse the snakes and scorpions represent demons and evil spirits. As Jesus says, we are given authority over them to overcome their power. This is very important in understanding deliverance. My purpose here is not to explain how to do deliverance, but to mention that we have the authority to deliver those afflicted and demonized, and break spiritual strongholds in Jesus name.

This authority is tied to faith, however. You need to be confident in who you are in Christ. Too often Christians will try to excerpt authority over the enemy only to be laughed at because the enemy knows that person has no real faith in who he is in Christ. Someone in the Bible who really understood authority was the centurion mentioned in Luke chapter seven. He went to see Jesus because his servant was sick and about to die. He told Jesus, "But say the word, and my servant will be healed." He told Jesus to just say the word because he understood authority and that this could be handled with authority. Jesus was amazed at the level of faith that the centurion had. Likewise, we need to have an understanding and faith in Jesus' authority, and then in our authority as his ambassadors. When a Christian states something in Jesus' name, it carries the same type of authority.

For example, sometimes a pain can come from an afflicting spirit. One time I prayed for a guy who said that he had pain in his ear. When I prayed, the pain dropped to his jaw. I prayed again and the pain moved to the back of his throat. Realizing this was an afflicting spirit, I commanded it go in Jesus name. The pain then left for good. It was interesting to me that the pain moved as I prayed, but didn't leave until I took authority (commanded it to go in Jesus name).

Of course, it can be a little more involved when it comes to bondages that need to be broken, which need deliverance. Those bondages can come from sinful patterns, believing lies of the enemy, words spoken over us, unforgiveness, generational curses, dealing with the occult, and more. In those cases, I would recommend seeking out someone experienced in handling those situations. However, true power is seen when using the tools that God provided us with, the authority in Jesus' name and the power the Holy Spirit gives. Too often I see Christians use tools that man gives (methods) and add a little Christian flavor to it. That's very limited in its power to break spiritual strongholds, and usually just manages them rather than break them.

Matthew 18:18 (NIV)
"Truly I tell you, whatever you bind on earth will be bound in heaven, and whatever you loose on earth will be loosed in heaven.

This verse speaks of our authority. We have been given authority over all bondages in Jesus name. We see this actually shown in Mark 7:33-35 where a man's ears are opened and a tongue is loosened.

> Mark 7:33-35 (NIV)
> After he took him aside, away from the crowd, Jesus put his fingers into the man's ears. Then he spit and touched the man's tongue. He looked up to heaven and with a deep sigh said to him, "Ephphatha!" (which means "Be opened!"). At this, the man's ears were opened, his tongue was loosened and he began to speak plainly.

I was at a conference where the speaker preaching said that he felt that we should pray for those with hearing problems. A lady in the row behind me got up, and those of us gathered around her, laid hands on her, and prayed. She looked to be in her sixties. So, it didn't surprise me that she had hearing problems. When we finished praying, everyone started going back to their seats, but I really felt the presence of God so I asked her if she noticed any difference. She took out her hearing aids and said no, there was no difference. So, I asked if I could pray again. I laid hands on her ears and prayed for healing. I felt the presence of God so strong my faith was really high. I asked again, but she said no change. Normally, I would I just stop and bless her at this point, but the presence of God was so strong I really expected some change. So, I asked her to tell me about when her hearing problems began. She said that ever since she was a little girl she has had hearing problems. She shared some medical background and trouble as a child with ears including blistering. Then she caught my attention with the next statement. She said that her mother said that she would have hearing problems the rest of her life. I immediately responded with asking if I could pray again. I said, "In Jesus name I break off the words spoken over you by your mother, and I command the spirit of deafness to go." She fell back into her seat which I didn't expect and felt bad about. Then she had this perplexed look on her face which turned to joy, and she said, "The roaring is gone." I didn't know what she was talking about because she never mentioned a roaring before this. The reason she needed the hearing aids was to amplify the sound over the roar she had heard in her ears.

That night it hit me how, unfortunately, we are sometimes careless with our words as well. Our words can often do tremendous damage. Proverbs 18:21 says we hold the power of life and death in our tongues. We need to be careful with our tongues. As James says, can fresh water and salt water flow from the same spring? If we want God to use us, we must learn to tame the tongue.

Thorns In the Flesh

The ministry of deliverance was important to Jesus from the beginning:

> Isaiah 61:1 (NIV)
> The Spirit of the Sovereign Lord is on me,
>   because the Lord has anointed me
>   to proclaim good news to the poor.
> He has sent me to **bind up the brokenhearted**,
>   to **proclaim freedom for the captives**
>   and **release from darkness for the prisoners**,

In the passage above we see God's heart to heal those with broken hearts, and set people free of their bondages. And what did Jesus tell the twelve disciples to do?

> Matthew 10:7-8 (NIV)
> As you go, proclaim this message: 'The kingdom of heaven has come near.' Heal the sick, raise the dead, cleanse those who have leprosy, **drive out demons**. Freely you have received; freely give.

To the seventy in Luke 10, He said the same thing, and to the church He said the same thing.

I should make it clear here that a Christian can be demonized in that they can be influenced in thought, influenced in behavior, and physically afflicted by demons. To help understand this, while the enemy has no access to the spirit of a Christian since it becomes joined by the Holy Spirit, the enemy still can afflict one's body physically and influence his soul's thoughts and emotions. Examples of afflictions to the body would be the deaf and dumb spirit mentioned in Mark 9:25 and the lady bent over from an afflicting spirit in Luke 13:11. A famous example of how Satan influences thought is in Matthew 16:23 when Jesus says to Peter, "Get behind me Satan."

Christians' emotions are also affected by the enemy. Many times I see Christians struggling with fear, anger, depression, or anxiety. These are opposite of the fruits of the Holy Spirit. They are the fruits of demonic spirits. Rather than try to deal with the symptoms, we need to learn to attack the source.

Ephesians 6:12 (NIV)
For our struggle is not against flesh and blood, but against the rulers, against the authorities, against the powers of this dark world and against the spiritual forces of evil in the heavenly realms.

As this verse points out, our struggles are not against flesh and blood, and that includes ourselves. Rather, these are spiritual attacks from the enemy. Too often people are trying to fix themselves, thinking that they are the problem. When in reality, they need to attack the spirit bringing this problem on.

Again, the great commission starts by saying what? All authority has been given to me in heaven and on earth, therefore... teaching them to observe (action) all things that I have commanded you ...

I never realized how much demonic activity there was around me until the Lord opened my eyes to it. I also started to run into it when

I starting praying for the sick. My purpose here is not to create any fear, but rather explain the importance of the authority that God has provided us in order to do His will.

There are times when one can just command a spirit of affliction to go, and it will leave. However, there are times when the spirits won't go so quickly because they have what many refer to as attachments (something to hold onto).

The enemy is very legalistic, and anytime he thinks he has a right he will use it. However, we need to know that through the work of the cross we have the ability to be set free of sin, bondages, and any grips of the enemy, but that's not always automatic. Sometimes people need more mature believers to coach them in how to walk in freedom.

God is primarily concerned with our spirit, then our soul, then our body. All battles against the enemy can be won by drawing from the power of Jesus' blood shed for us at the cross. Both sin and Satan can no longer have a hold on us that we can't break free from.

However, we can be afflicted when we open doors to the enemy by dabbling in things we shouldn't or have persistent sin in our lives. It could also be due to generational curses or curses spoken over a person. The enemy takes advantage of such things. However, by God's grace we can always experience deliverance with an adjustment in our hearts and actions.

Note that the arrival of Paul's thorn follows him stating all his accomplishments and experiences. So, we know why this spirit showed up (pride). It was an afflicting spirit. I would never have been able to understand the passage of Paul's thorn properly until I started doing deliverance ministry.

2 Corinthians 12:7-9 (NIV)

or because of these surpassingly great revelations. Therefore, **in order to keep me from becoming conceited**, I was **given a thorn in my flesh**, a **messenger of Satan**, to torment me. Three times I pleaded with the Lord to take it away from me. But he said to me, "**My grace is sufficient for you**, for my power is made perfect in weakness." Therefore I will boast all the more gladly about my weaknesses, so that Christ's power may rest on me.

The passage on Paul's thorn in the flesh is very small, and not much detail is provided. It provides insight to the fact that God cares more about our hearts than our bodies. That's not to say he doesn't care about our bodies though. Paul prayed three times for the thorn to be removed, and God's reply was, "My grace is sufficient for you." So, the big question is what does "my grace is sufficient" mean?

Let me first start by saying that God's ultimate desire would be for Paul's issue of pride to be removed and the afflicting spirit to be removed as well. This is what total deliverance looks like.

That being said, I would propose that Paul had the ability, by God's grace, to work it out himself with the power of the Holy Spirit. Again, the Bible isn't clear whether the spirit ever left. I believe by God's grace, He has given us authority over the demonic. So, Paul needed deliverance, but there was a heart issue that needed to be dealt with first.

The first question is, by God's grace, can Paul's thorn be healed by the work of the Holy Spirit? The answer is yes. Nothing is too big for God as long as the will of the man is engaged.

The second question then is, after Paul's pride issue would be dealt with, would there be any reason Paul couldn't command the spirit to leave by the authority that God gave him? No, there is no reason at that point that Paul couldn't just command the spirit to leave by the authority of who he is in Christ.

Sometimes when we pray for something to be taken away, God shows grace in His answer in a way that is different than what we asked for. An example of this is when God sent the fiery snakes into the wilderness after the Israelites complained too much. They asked God to take them away, but He didn't. Instead He provided a way for healing by having Moses build a bronze snake and put it on a pole. If they looked with faith at the snake, they were healed.

When God said to Paul, "My grace is sufficient for you," that grace had to enable something. I'm sure it enabled Paul to endure the torment while he had it, but I believe it was reflective of God providing Paul the tools he needed in order to be healed of it all (pride and affliction) as well.

God's desire for Paul was for his pride to be dealt with. The Bible doesn't say that Paul continued to struggle with pride. However, I believe if and when Paul reached victory in the area of pride, he would also be able to have victory over the afflicting spirit. The point is God's grace is sufficient to accomplish both.

It should be noted that all along, Paul has the presence of God to bring victory over spirits. As I mentioned already, the presence of God was on him so much that he could even send a handkerchief that he rubbed on himself to drive evil spirits out (Acts 19:11-12). However, the persistent pride allowed the spirit afflicting him to have an "attachment" so to speak.

If I were to summarize the whole experience, I would say it's always God's will for us to live healthy in spirit, soul, and body. It is also God's will for us to have victory over the enemy. However, when there is a heart issue that needs to be corrected, in His mercy, He doesn't bring victory over the enemy (afflicting spirit) until we receive healing of the heart issue. I have seen this first hand when involved in deliverance experiences. If the deliverance becomes a power encounter only, where by God's authority, I see the evil spirit leave, he will be right back later if the heart issue isn't dealt with. Once the heart issue is dealt with, the spirit is easy to get rid of.

A problem I have seen, though, is when Christians get in their minds that God is bringing affliction or sickness on them to teach them something. First of all, sickness is of the devil and part of the curse of the earth after the fall. Yes, sin can be the cause of sickness. However, if sin is the cause of the sickness, it will either be obvious to us, or God would reveal it. It frustrates me to hear Christians say, "God must be teaching me something though this sickness," and they can't even say what it is (of course because He isn't). God doesn't use sickness to teach us or develop character. Instead, we may have opened the door to attack with our sin. Examples of this would be dabbling in the occult, drugs, or pornography or perhaps harboring unforgiveness. One may also have a direct result of sickness due to sin, such as with sexually transmitted disease. However, that is not God striking you with the disease; it's simply a cause and effect situation. Secondly, afflicting spirits are fallen angels, and deliverance is needed because of what Satan and his workers are doing, not God.

We see clearly in the Bible that God is more concerned about the soul and spirit than our physical well-being. He cares about that also, but there are priorities. For example, Jesus says in Mark 9 if your hand causes you to sin, to cut it off, if your foot causes you to sin to, cut it off, and if your eye causes you to sin, pluck it out because it is better for you to enter life maimed, crippled, or without an eye than to be thrown into hell. He doesn't actually mean to do this, but He shows the seriousness of your spiritual state relative to your physical.

I have seen multiple times where God, in His grace, will sometimes not bring deliverance of an afflicting spirit to heal a deeper issue, and that issue isn't even always sin. Sometimes it's believing a lie, such as "I'm not worthy of healing." Anytime you believe a lie of the enemy you empower him.

This subject is too large to completely cover here, and my intent is not to make this a how-to book. Rather I want to help Christians realize who they are in Christ and what they have access to. We need to understand that we carry authority, and we need to learn how to be effective with that authority.

As ambassadors, our authority is executed in Jesus name. This is a name above all names at which every knee will bow according to Philippians 2:9, 10. This is because, according to verse 7, Jesus humbled himself in obedience to God and died a criminal's death on a cross. It all comes back to what Jesus did on the cross. That is the point of victory that we fight from.

How to Live a Life of Righteousness

We need to live in a manner worthy of representing Christ not just in power, but in righteousness. While we don't earn any giftings or mantels, we need a heart that matches our hands.

In Romans 7, Paul says he couldn't live a righteous life as a Pharisee (on his own discipline), but thanks be to Jesus who rescued him from this body of death.

It is by God's grace we are saved, and it is by God's grace we can live a victorious life over the bondage of sin.

Many times a person can't receive physical healing until he sees himself worthy of it. He needs to view himself correctly. The same type of identity issue keeps some in bondage to sin. They need to see who they are in Christ to have victory. They need to see themselves as powerful, pure in God's sight, and a new creation.

People are largely influenced by how they view themselves. I'm not talking about positive thinking. I'm talking about proper thinking. The Bible says that when you are saved you are a new creation.

Therefore, if anyone is in Christ, he is a new creation; old things have passed away; behold, all things have become new.

Satan wants you to look at yourself as the same old defeated person, but the truth is you now have a new nature that desires to do good, and the Holy Spirit lives within you to help you overcome sin.

So, how does this play out in our lives? How do we live a victorious life – that overcomes the bondage to sin? Well, first of all, we need to know we can't just muster up the willpower to do it. Satan would love for you to just work at it on your own and make you feel like a failure because you continue in your sinful ways.

It needs to start with an adjustment of the source (desires), which is the heart. If our heart is going after the wrong desires, we will fail.

James 1:14 (NIV)
But each person is tempted when they are dragged away by their own evil desire and enticed.

The problem is our heart gets too full of the things of this world, even when not sinful (i.e. the American dream). Jesus said in Matthew 6:33, "Seek first the Kingdom of God and His righteousness..."

When we become friendly with the things of this world, and we choose them over God, we are being unfaithful to Him. See, when you accept Christ into your life, you are moving into a covenant relationship with Him. So, when we choose to be unfaithful to Him, the picture would be that of an affair in a marriage. So, if we use that analogy, it helps us understand how to live unstained by the world as James puts it (James 1:27).

The Bible never really teaches to work at not sinning now that you are a Christian. That's because not sinning is a result of who you are in Christ. So, if you have a sin issue in your life, work on your relationship with Jesus. In spiritual warfare Satan wants you to focus on him. Then your focus is off of Christ or what God wants you to be doing. The Bible says to pursue God. If you focus on God, the enemy will be defeated, not if you focus on the enemy. It all, and I mean all, comes back to relationship.

Fear has some power as a motivator to do right, but you are just managing with fear. Love is way more powerful, even to the point where the Bible says that perfect love casts out all fear.

If I want to make my marriage affair-proof, there are certain guards I can put in place. However, the most powerful thing I can do is work to strengthen my marriage. Then when I may be tempted to be unfaithful, my desire to remain faithful to my wife is much stronger.

People who have affairs typically are unsatisfied with their spouse. I'm not saying this is an excuse. I'm saying that when one loves their spouse, they don't consider doing something that would hurt them, and they don't look to others to fill their needs.

It's the same with God when He is your desire. The attraction of the things offered by this world tends to fade. If I work on my relationship with God, that sensitivity to sin grows. In fact, as you get closer to God, you get much more sensitive to the Holy Spirit, who lives in you. He will make you very uncomfortable when you force Him to journey with you as you sin. As you learn to walk in the Spirit, the desires of the world fade, and even when they pop up, your spirit will be troubled by the Holy Spirit if you contemplate sinning.

There have been times when I just thought about sinning that I felt like I was going to have a heart attack. This is not due to a fear that has come on me. This comes from the presence of the Holy Spirit in my life. I'm not saying this in arrogance, but to illustrate the reality of walking in the Spirit. We need to remember that the Holy Spirit experiences what we do. If you attempt to do something that will grieve Him, it should be quite uncomfortable for you.

The goal is to abide in Christ. However, it's more than just acting in accordance with Him. We want to abide in a way that our thoughts are to mirror His thoughts. Our heart is to mirror His heart. We are to begin to feel about things as He feels. We are to desire things that He desires. The only way that happens is, like any other relationship, by spending time with Him - letting our minds be renewed and letting our hearts be transformed.

True repentance needs to affect your head (renewing of the mind, changing the way you think about things), your heart (loving God too much to be ok with just letting grace abound), and your feet (result in a change of action). It's like food that starts with the mouth, moves to the stomach, and enables the feet. Likewise, by God's grace, repentance starts in our mind, moves to the heart, and affects our walk.

It all starts by changing our view of God, sin, and ourselves. It's not about what we do or don't do that forms our identity. It's about what Jesus did that defines who we are. While the status of our communication within our relationship can be hindered until we confess our sin and make things right again, our identity never changes.

The enemy is always trying to attack our identity because he knows we will act according to how we view ourselves. We're not just sinners saved by grace or beggars telling other beggars where to get food. The Bible says that the Holy Spirit is conforming us to the image of Christ. He's conforming us to a son or daughter by whom we cry Abba, Father. He's sanctifying us so that we reflect the title we have of saint and helping us realize the Father's love that is poured out on us, so we will accept the reality of our new identity.

Lastly, while the Holy Spirit corrects us, He doesn't condemn us. Any feeling of condemnation is from the enemy. The Bible is clear that God is the God of reconciliation. After our failures we need to move closer to Him, not let them push us farther away. He's not scary. He's a loving Father desiring reconciliation, and His Spirit is there to help us be overcomers.

Tradition, Experience, and God's Word

We are often warned against experience-based theology. However, I would say people are more affected by their lack of experience. So, often they bend their beliefs to match or justify their lack of experience.

Sometimes a person will have a bad experience that will keep him from going to church and even being a Christian. Likewise, a Christian can have a bad experience that keeps him from revival.

Jesus was rejected by many Jews, even scholars (those who studied the scriptures) because Jesus didn't look like the Messiah they were looking for or expecting. They had a picture of the Messiah that was probably taught from one generation to the next. When Jesus came, they missed their Messiah because they couldn't accept that image of the Messiah. Likewise, we have Christians praying for revival that are missing it because it doesn't look like what they expected.

There are times God doesn't explain everything. But too often we aren't willing to accept something or be a part of something until we have it all figured out. But the truth is, we are called to obedience, even when it doesn't all make sense to us. Our lack of understanding will not be an excuse.

In John 15, it talks about bearing much fruit, and that's not internal fruit, but external fruit. And this fruit God is talking about, you can't accomplish on your own.

With a cessationist point of view (that many of the spiritual gifts, signs, and wonders have ceased), much of the Bible really isn't written for us, including much of the great commission. In the great commission, Jesus says, "Teaching to do the things I have commanded you." In some seminaries today, they are not teaching the things that the disciples were taught to do: heal the sick, cast out demons, and preach the gospel of the kingdom (we only do part of this - salvation). Our seminaries tend to teach things that don't require faith to achieve. Yet, without faith it is impossible to please God (Hebrews 11:6). We say we are called to be like Christ, but we teach that in only trying not to sin and be nice to people. So, what does it mean to be called to be like Christ?

Let me give a bit of a satire-type example. I know I've heard some people can hit a baseball 300 feet. But, in general, man can't hit that way. I mean no one in my church that I know of has ever hit a baseball 300 feet. So, I'm just saying to be careful because it just sounds strange to me. I mean don't get me wrong, if God wanted me to hit baseball 300 feet, I know it could happen.

Those who preach the gifts listed in 1 Corinthians 12 are not for today are robbing Christians of some of their inheritance and discouraging them from going after what God intended for them. It's like telling somebody who's not kicked a field goal or not hit a homerun, "Hey you're not gifted" or "Hey, you don't have what it takes," "You are not coordinated enough," or "That just doesn't happen anymore." They're stealing their hope, and they're stealing their confidence. The big difference is one can look at somebody and say well they're not going to be able to hit a homerun 300 feet, but he can't say that about the gifts of the Spirit because it's not about us. It's about the Holy Spirit doing work in us, and He is made strong in our weakness. In fact, He loves to use the least qualified for His greater glory. If we just focus on what God hasn't done instead of what He has done, it will destroy our faith and destroy everything that we can do effectively for the kingdom. It's a lie from the enemy.

Cease means to cease. That is, not exist anymore, period. Why is it so important to some preachers to have to preach that something doesn't exist anymore? Do they feel they need to come up with a doctrine that justifies their personal lack of experience? It's like telling Moses, "Hey, you've got to be careful because the other Israelites have never experienced what you're doing," and they see the magicians do the same thing.

As we see revival rising, which we're seeing now, we are also going to see an increase in the spirit of anti-Christ moving. We see it not just in the non-Christians, but more often in Christians. It doesn't mean they're not saved. It doesn't mean they're not good people on a human standard. But just as Peter spoke to Jesus, and Jesus replied, "Get behind me Satan," people can be influenced by demonic thought.

While out to lunch with a colleague one day, he said that he's asked people, "How do you know that God is real?" The conclusion that he came to, and I agree with, was that the best proof is an experience. It is not because of some really good argument, but an experience of how God changed somebody. However, the lack of experience is never a good argument for something not existing. For me to say that it is impossible for someone to hit a baseball 300 feet because I've never personally done it is foolish.

We need to get back to believing God's Word. That statement may be offensive to some, but it's really true.

> Psalm 106:20-25
> Thus they changed their glory
> Into the image of an ox that eats grass.
> They forgot God their Savior,
> Who had done great things in Egypt,
> Wondrous works in the land of Ham,
> Awesome things by the Red Sea.
> Therefore He said that He would destroy them,
> Had not Moses His chosen one stood before Him in the breach,
> To turn away His wrath, lest He destroy them.
> Then they despised the pleasant land;
> They did not believe His word,
> But complained in their tents,
> And did not heed the voice of the Lord.

I'm not one who cries easily, but when I read this passage one morning while having my quiet time, I started weeping.

In verses 21 and 22 we see they forgot testimonies of great things, wonderful things, and awesome things. In verse 24 we see that they despised their pleasant land, and they didn't believe His Word. In verse 25 they complained. They complained to God because they blamed Him for everything wrong.

I felt the Holy Spirit say to me, "This is the church of America." When we don't believe God's word, we create false doctrine, we create false gods, and we complain.

I asked God, how did we create false gods? When we change the focus of our hearts and our confidence, we create a false God. Ever think about what the calf was made out of? It was made of gold. Yes, their form of idolatry was different, but it was of the same substance.

The verse that really got me was verse 25. They complained. Much too often, whenever something goes wrong the first one blamed is God. See many Christians blame God for everything, including their sickness. In the meantime, the devil is literally getting away with murder.

Let's get back to believing God's Word! Since the beginning, all the pain and suffering we experience comes from man not believing what God said. Instead man listened to the devil as he made him question God's Word. "Did God really say …?"

Christians have been given their authority back at a very high price, but they listen to Satan saying, "Does God really mean…?" Satan says, "That's not for you", and sadly many have created doctrines that excuse God's Word away. This time we have no excuse because God wrote it down for us. Yet, we tend to give Adam a hard time.

Many Christians are praying for revival, yet they're not willing to admit that they're spiritually dead. Revival by definition means to bring life back into something. Then when they see it, it freaks them out, and they reject it. The truth is that if we just got back to the basics of the Bible, we would be fine. God just wants His people to believe what He says.

Revelation 19:10
"… the testimony of Jesus is the spirit of prophecy."

A testimony is a declaration of something that has been done in the past. Prophecy states what will be done in the future. Many use this passage to teach on the power of the testimony. That is, once you see or hear of a testimony, or better yet, you experience it yourself, it builds faith for the next time you are faced with that situation. For example, the faith I needed once when I experienced a cancerous tumor that dissolved in my hand was based on someone else's testimony that had experienced the same thing previously.

I'm going to take a different approach on this scripture, but similar meaning. The testimony of Jesus Christ is what Jesus did, how He did it, and what He said (prophesied) specifically about us (His followers or disciples). God just wants His people to believe what He says, and then act on it.

We know that Jesus moved in power, healed the sick, cast out demons, and more. He did this by the same Holy Spirit that we are anointed with. That is why we are called Christians (little anointed ones). Then He said we will do the same and more.

John 14:12
"Most assuredly, I say to you, he who believes in Me, the works that I do he will do also; and greater works than these he will do, because I go to My Father.

The correlation of us doing the works He did and He returning to the Father is that He needed to return to the Father in order to send us the Holy Spirit.

Revival is coming, and when it does, we will do the things Jesus said we would.

Psalm 119:88
Revive me according to Your loving kindness,
So that I may keep the testimony of Your mouth.

Revival comes through His loving kindness, and when revival hits us our love tanks will overflow and we will do what Jesus prophesied that we would, all that He did and more.

The Spirit
of Anti-Christ

Satan isn't afraid of Christians who don't know who they are. His fear is revival, but what does that mean? By definition revival means to bring life back into something. As Christians we have lost our life source (not literally) in that we have grown weak. What has changed is our focus and our view of ourselves. We pursue what we don't need to pursue, and we don't pursue the things we should.

> Matthew 6:25-33 (NIV)
> "Therefore I tell you, do not worry about your life, what you will eat or drink; or about your body, what you will wear. Is not life more than food, and the body more than clothes? Look at the birds of the air; they do not sow or reap or store away in barns, and yet your heavenly Father feeds them. Are you not much more valuable than they? Can any one of you by worrying add a single hour to your life? "And why do you worry about clothes? See how the flowers of the field grow. They do not labor or spin. Yet I tell you that not even Solomon in all his splendor was dressed like one of these. If that is how God clothes the grass of the field, which is here today and tomorrow is thrown into the fire, will he not much more clothe you—you of little faith? So do not worry, saying, 'What shall we eat?' or 'What shall we drink?' or 'What shall we wear?'

For the pagans run after all these things, and your h_
Father knows that you need them. But seek first his kingdom
and his righteousness, and all these things will be given to
you as well.

Jesus said seek the Kingdom of God. I find that many Christians
don't even know what that means. They think that is just being involved
in ministry or in the church. So, first of all, they need to understand
that the church and the Kingdom of God are two different things. The
church is what God wants to work through. The Kingdom of God is
where God resides and rules. We are in the church, but the kingdom
is in us. Of course, God's kingdom on earth will not be fully realized
until He returns, but we can provide tastes of His kingdom here on
earth in the meantime.

Secondly, Paul says to pursue spiritual gifts. To many this may
seem wrong. It is, if your motive is wrong, but if you are trying to live
an effective life that will give God the glory He deserves, you need
them. Instead, we are pursuing in action and in prayer our security
and needs which we are told not to worry about.

We tend to align doctrine that will match our experience, primarily when there is a lack of experience. Usually, without knowing
it, this doctrine is demonically inspired. I know that is a strong and
offensive statement, but the spirit of anti-Christ is against Christ,
which means anointed one. The spirit of anti-Christ is against the
anointing. So, how does the spirit of anti-Christ stop the anointing?
It can't, unless we let it by not realizing who we are as Christians
(little anointed ones).

The other thing that the enemy does is create fear in us when we
don't understand something. As it says in Isaiah 55:9, God's thoughts
are much higher than ours. God doesn't always make sense to us, and
He doesn't have to.

When I, or others I know, pray for healing, I see things that will make you wonder all the time. For example, why would God allow me to control how much arch is in a foot rather than just make it perfect? Why would God allow someone's leg to grow out too far while the person praying for it to grow out is slightly distracted? Why would Jesus need to ask if the man's sight was perfect, and then need to lay hands on his eyes again?

Some say that everything God does needs to make sense. I would like to respond, "Make sense to whom? Does everything that God does need to make sense to you? If so, who are you to think that God needs to only do things that make sense to you?"

How much of the New Testament applies to us? When we start to say that some of what is in the New Testament is not for us today, we start down a dangerous slippery slope. I understand majoring on the majors and minoring on the minors, but when we take away the power of the Holy Spirit and say that's not for today, that's huge. Not only does that strip us of power, it's not a complete gospel. It's not the gospel of the kingdom that Jesus told us to preach. We tend to preach the gospel of salvation. I'm not saying there always has to be a supernatural event in the sense of us seeing it that way. However, when one realizes the truth when hearing the gospel and gives his life to Christ, it is a supernatural event. It is not due to a manipulation of a man-made method. Paul even said he did not persuade with words but with the power of the Holy Spirit (paraphrased).

I'm realizing that for me to be a disciple of Christ, it needs to look the same as the disciples in the Bible. If I'm afraid of getting out of my comfort zone, then I'm not willing to take up my cross and follow Jesus.

So, what does it look like to pursue or desire the spiritual gifts? Some will say, "Well, I asked for it, and it didn't happen." Then they just gave up. They don't know what desire looks like. The kingdom of

God is like a merchant seeking fine pearls (Matthew 13:45). How far are you willing to go to get the desire of your heart? The answer to that question will tell you about the size of your desire.

It all comes down to the renewing of the mind. It's there that the battle takes place. But an anti-Christ spirit opposes the truth and hinders the full transformation. It all comes down to identity. The enemy attacks your identity to inhibit you. It's the same spirit that blinded the Pharisees from seeing who Jesus is that is blinding people today as to who we are in Christ. The teaching that we no longer have power is demonic and totally denies the work of the Holy Spirit.

It's been my experience that where someone doesn't understand something he will often make fun of it. No doubt examples can be found of abuse. Anything good is often abused and counterfeited. It has also been my experience that when something isn't understood it brings fear. You can see this in Mark 4:35-41 when Jesus calms the storm. The disciples were afraid in the storm, but when Jesus calms the storm, it says they feared exceedingly. The same is true today. When life's storms come, in the form of an incurable disease for example, people become afraid. However, if God offers a solution to that storm in a way that they don't understand, their fear will sometimes keep them in the storm because they are even more afraid of the solution.

So often I hear people say, "Well, you need to be careful." Careful of what? Look at the fruit. Does it bring glory to God? Does it bring the person ministered to closer to Christ? Does it bring you closer to Christ? This is how you determine the source. I understand the new age movement. Look if we (the church) don't start showing our power, then people will be drawn to the counterfeit.

The problem is the anti-Christ spirit has gotten the church so afraid of the supernatural they throw it all in one bucket. To which I will say, "Be careful." Be careful because I have seen too many times where the work of the Holy Spirit is attributed to the work of the devil. This was simply done because they couldn't explain it. They have never seen the supernatural. So, they assume it's of the devil. It's the same thing the Pharisees did with Jesus when He was on earth, and Jesus called this blasphemy of the Holy Spirit.

I once got in a discussion with a brother in Christ on how Jesus did His miracles through the Holy Spirit and not by the fact that He was God. The next morning was the only time I actually heard the audible voice of God. He simply said "Blasphemy of the Holy Spirit." I immediately knew what that meant. I went straight to the Bible and looked up the passage in Matthew 12. As the passage makes very clear, Jesus did the miracles as a man through the Holy Spirit, and He warned against attributing those miracles to the devil. My purpose of sharing this is not to place fear into anyone that they may have committed an unforgivable sin, which is rejecting Christ and attributing His works accomplished by the Holy Spirit to the devil. My purpose in stating this story is to warn that anytime you attribute the work of the Holy Spirit to the devil, it has got to be very grieving to God.

Fresh Wine Skins and
a New Generation

When I was younger, I remember many older people would say to me, "I sure wish I was your age and know what I know now." Well, I now catch myself saying that to those younger than I, for what God has revealed to them at such a young age.

It has become apparent to me as I observe this new revival movement that God is primarily focusing on the youth. It's as if the older generation has quenched the Holy Spirit by being choosy on what they will accept. Don't get me wrong, there have been some revivals in the past. However, the fact is that God sometimes does things through his Holy Spirit that old wine skins will not accept.

> Mark 2:22
> And no one puts new wine into old wineskins; or else the new wine bursts the wineskins, the wine is spilled, and the wineskins are ruined. But new wine must be put into new wineskins."

There are times God doesn't explain everything, but too often we aren't willing to accept something or be a part of something until we have it all figured out. Yet the truth is that we are called to obedience, even when it doesn't all make sense to us. Our lack of understanding will not be an excuse.

Many leaders in this new movement focus on pouring into the youth. This is partially because they are our future, but also because God made it clear to them that the youth are to be the focus.

However, the youth need leadership. What they need are Calebs and Joshuas. If you are of the older generation and you want to be a part of the new season of how God is moving, take heart, you can play a vital role in this new revival. I was initially saddened when at a conference the speaker would get us all so excited about what God was doing, and then he would ask the youth to come forward to be prayed for. I thought, "Hey, that's not fair, what about me?" However, I got really excited when God showed me in His word that I have a key role to play, as I believe many others in my generation do as well. God spoke to me out of Joshua 11:14 where Caleb is speaking to Joshua.

> Joshua 14:11 (NIV)
> I am still as strong today as the day Moses sent me out; I'm just as vigorous to go out to battle now as I was then.

While all of the generation of Caleb and Joshua died in the wilderness, Joshua and Caleb were not only allowed to go into the Promised Land, but they didn't age like their peers. As I read that, I felt God tell me that I still have a good portion of my life to live in revival. Praise the Lord, what a blessing!

When the twelve spies were sent into the Promised Land, they came back with a report of the awesome fruit and also a report of fear. These days we can see the awesome fruit of what the Spirit of the Lord is doing, but there is also a fear of being wrong that will inhibit the acceptance of anything new of God, at least that is new to us. As a result, we have a generation that is enjoying some of the lesser blessings of God as the Israelites did in the wilderness, but we are missing out on the greater promises of what God intended for us.

The big difference is that it's not too late. If you were like me, you didn't know there was more. Now that you know, why wouldn't you do whatever it takes to attain it? I should warn, however, that there is a cost. For those who receive much, much will be expected. So, first you need to decide, are you going to live for yourself or for God? Are you all in, or trying to hold on to your life as much as you can, so to speak?

The Real Life

Remember those old beer commercials that would say, "This is the life," and they would show some nice event like fishing or something else relaxing or fun? The truth is, that as Jesus said, He is the life. He is the creator and giver of life. He also says that He has come to give life more abundantly (John 10:10). Then in Matthew 16:25, Jesus makes a very interesting statement: "For whoever wants to save their life will lose it, but whoever loses their life for me will find it."

Many Christians are living the American dream with the security of eternal life. On the surface that may sound great, but it is very short sighted. They base their blessings on a nice job, family, health, etc., but these are all insignificant to the blessing of eternal life. I'm not saying to not count those as blessings and be thankful, but we don't often realize what God has really provided for us through the death of His Son. Salvation isn't cheap. It's a free gift to us, but the price was extremely high for God. If we really understood what we've been given, to complain about anything is an insult to God. We would think it to be ridiculous for us to go on and on complaining to a doctor of the pain of getting poked by a needle when getting a shot because it's relatively a short period of time. However, what we don't grasp is that this life is infinitesimally small compared to eternal life. Yet we too often judge God on this little spec in our timeline of life. We also tend to place most of our time and energy on this very short season here on earth on the wrong things. The intended Christian life mind-set is long term in its thinking. It focuses on laying up treasures in heaven –where they won't get stolen or rusted (Matthew 6:19).

However, many Christians believe that their goal in life is to just try to live a moral life and experience the American dream until they go to heaven. The problem with that is that it's hard to pursue the American dream and be a true disciple of Christ at that same time. The reason is that the American dream is all about comfort. In contrast, being a disciple of Christ means to take up your cross which is not an emblem of comfort. While the two may exist at some level, it's the pursuit that's the issue because it's all about the heart. That is why Jesus said seek first the Kingdom of God.

Too often we are afraid to take risk because of how it will make us look. We like our comfort zones. Then we wonder why we never suffer persecution, at all. That's because too often we aren't living a life worthy of it. The enemy isn't going to waste his time opposing the spiritually dead. But if Christians are having an impact for God's Kingdom, I can guarantee the enemy will try to oppose them. It's like in a war; you place your troops where one kingdom is attacking the other, and we are living in war. However, take courage because the church has been equipped for victory.

> Matthew 16:18 (NIV)
> ".. and on this rock I will build my church, and the gates of Hades will not overcome it."

Note that in the verse above it says the gates of hades (hell in some translations). The point is that it's not the church's gates that will not prevail, but it's hell's gates. The church has the power to break into the other kingdom and set the captives free. However, as with any war, there is sacrifice involved.

When Paul says I die daily, he is talking about sacrifice he has given for the Christian life. The question is, would you trade some of the difficulties he experienced (beaten with rods, pelted with stones, shipwrecked, constantly on the move, often gone without sleep, often gone without food, …) for your peaceful life to experience some of the awesome things he experienced?

I think that's the tradeoff we are faced with. If you want to do something significant for God, you can expect three things: lots of joy, a large sense of significance, and lots of spiritual warfare.

Many people really don't want to be a disciple of Christ because it's uncomfortable. However, if you choose not to serve God because you're afraid of being uncomfortable, it's a worse choice in the end as far as comfort goes because you're going to be way more uncomfortable when you're standing before God at the end of your life and have nothing but poor excuses.

You can choose to be content with the American dream and walk in the spiritual wilderness. Or, you can say, "I'm all in God," and live the adventure. The adventure will bring pain, persecution, discomfort, and attack. But the blessings and the spoils of the fight are well worth it. Jesus said to count the cost because there is one. But to live as a real man or woman of God, to experience God working through you, to taste the Kingdom that is not fully realized, is so worth it.

Appendix: Spiritual Gifts of 1 Corinthians 12:8-10

When discussing the gifts listed in 1 Corinthians 12:8-10, I realize that there is a large misunderstanding of what these gifts are. I find this almost amusing as those who are adamant that these gifts are no longer active often don't even understand what they are.

For those not familiar with all the spiritual gifts listed in the Bible, it should be noted that this is not a complete list of all gifts. There are more gifts listed in Romans 12:6-8, 1 Corinthians 12:28, Ephesians 4:11, and 1 Peter 4:11. However, I'm covering the ones in 1 Corinthians 12:8-10 here because they are the least understood. These gifts are not talents or natural abilities, but rather supernatural abilities given by the Holy Spirit. As verse 7 puts it, these are the manifestation of the Spirit.

The word of wisdom: This is where the Holy Spirit gives supernatural insight and wisdom in what to do in a specific situation. An example of where this is very helpful is when one is faced with a situation that is unique or new to him, and the Holy Spirit gives him wisdom in what to do in that situation beyond his natural wisdom.

The word of knowledge: This is when the Holy Spirit gives supernatural knowledge of something that the person receiving this knowledge couldn't have known if the Holy Spirit didn't reveal it. An example of this is when Jesus meets the woman at the well and tells her about her life. Words of knowledge can come in multiple forms. For example, I often get words of knowledge for healing in the form of feeling someone else's pain, and this is the Holy Spirit revealing something physically about a person that needs prayer. It's learning to hear His still small voice. Many move in this gift and don't even know it.

The gift of faith: This goes beyond normal faith and is important for those called to a ministry that is especially difficult. This gifting also allows for greater miracles when praying. One thing I would like to note is that all measures of faith are a gift. However, faith can also be strengthened through exercise. The more you work it out, the stronger it will become.

Gifts of healing: I believe these are among the most misunderstood gifts. To start with, let me point out that it is gifts of healing (plural), not gift of healing. So, they are associated with different types of sicknesses and diseases. There are also different degrees of gifting in this area just like not all are gifted at the same level for teaching or evangelism. Just because someone has a gift of healing doesn't mean that everyone will be healed when he prays for him, just like an evangelist doesn't lead everyone to salvation. There are many factors involved in both of those situations.

One of the main issues I find that people have with those with gifts of healing is that they think that if God wants to heal them then He just will. They don't need someone in particular to pray for them. Personally, if I have a severe sickness that I can't find a solution to, but I hear of a place that does, I'd go there. I've seen people do this for special medical treatments, but, sadly, too often they won't for prayer. I believe this is a pride issue as well as a misunderstanding of the gifts. There is something humbling to go to someone for prayer, especially when it's not someone in your own church. It reminds me of the story of Naaman, the commander of the army who had leprosy (2 Kings 5). He was told by Elisha the prophet to wash in the Jordan seven times, and Naaman was furious that he had to do that. Not only did he need to wash in the river seven times, he couldn't do it in his river of choice. He did ultimately obey, however, and got healed. It's interesting seeing the result of Naaman getting healed. He believed in the one true God (2 Kings 5:15) and stopped sacrificing to idols (2 Kings 5:17). Healing is beneficial for more than just the physical result. Ideally, you want it to change how a person thinks, whether they are a Christian or not. A gift of healing, like all the other gifts, becomes stronger as it is exercised.

The working of miracles: This gift refers to the working of miracles outside of healing. An example would be the multiplication of food when needed. I have heard of this among missionaries these days who serve in areas of great poverty. Another example would be when Elijah calls fire down from heaven (1 Kings 18). In this case it should be noted that this is a specific type of instance that brings glory to the Lord and revelation of truth to many misled by a god empowered by the demonic. Miracles are never for the purpose of just showing off.

The gift of prophecy: This involves speaking to a person or group of people something God is saying to them. This is not to be held at the same level as the written Word of God, but serves a specific purpose in that it is personal and encouraging. The difference between this gift and that of psychics is the source of the information. Remember Satan is the great counterfeiter. His psychics are trying to imitate what those with the gift of prophecy can do.

Discerning of spirits: This is a gift that allows discerning those moving in the supernatural as well as the spirits themselves. Demons will at times try to pass themselves off as angels, and those moving in the power of the demonic may try to pass themselves off as men of God. Those with this gift will quickly discern the truth of the source of that spirit. As a side note, when in doubt just ask the person or spirit who Jesus is to them, and the truth will be revealed. The demonic can't lie in this case. No one can say that Jesus is Lord accept by the Holy Spirit (1 Corinthians 12:3).

Different types of tongues: This is the ability to supernaturally speak or understand a different language that one would otherwise not know.

The interpretation of tongues: This is the supernatural ability to understand a message from the Holy Spirit spoken by someone else.

About the author

Steve Dominguez is an author and speaker who has trained others in living out the Christian life in power. He and his wife, Risa, have a passion for the revival of God's church. They have both served in a variety of ministries including healing and deliverance. Steve has also followed in his father's footsteps in jail ministry which he has been involved with for almost 30 years.

You may contact Steve Dominguez at Steve.Rock63@gmail.com

Made in the USA
Monee, IL
27 August 2019